THE DARK ARTS OF IMMORTALITY:

Transformation through War, Sex, & Magic

Ross G. H. Shott

authorHOUSE

1663 Liberty Drive, Suite 200
Bloomington, Indiana 47403
(800) 839-8640
www.AuthorHouse.com

© 2005 Ross G. H. Shott. All Rights Reserved.

No part of this book may be reproduced, stored in a retrieval system, or transmitted by any means without the written permission of the author.

First published by AuthorHouse 09/21/05

ISBN: 1-4208-8054-3 (sc)

Printed in the United States of America
Bloomington, Indiana

This book is printed on acid-free paper.

Table of Contents

Dedication vii

Introduction ix

I. Preliminaries 1

II. Reality Check 11

III. Cycle of Interaction 35

IV. Left Hand Path 55

V. Divine Paradigm 69

VI. Self-Evolution Theory 85

VII. Hidden Powers 93

VIII. Art of War 111

IX. Art of Sex 125

X. Art of Magic 141

XI. Synergy 155

XII. Conclusions 163

Bibliography 167

FIGURES

Illustrated by Torvald Adolphson

Figure 1. Interactive Universe
(Chapter II)

Figure 2. Cycle of Interaction
(Chapter III)

Figure 3. Self-complex
(Chapter VI)

Figure 4. Chaos symbol
(Chapter VIII)

Figure 5. Pentacle Symbol
(Chapter IX)

Figure 6. Valknut Symbol
(Chapter X)

Figure 7. States of Being
(Chapter XI)

Dedicated

To the

Lasting memory

&

Enduring fame

Of the

Harii

Introduction

All the business of war, and indeed all the business of life,
is to endeavour to find out what you don't know
by what you do;
  —Duke of Wellington

If you had the power within your reach to insure your own immortality, would you risk all to grasp it? Think about it. No longer would you plead for the mercy of others. No longer would you bow to invisible masters. No longer would you struggle for table scraps. You could become master of your own destiny. You could become as God.

The Dark Arts of Immortality: Transformation through War, Sex, and Magic is that "power" and you have it in your "grasp" right now. Few activities occupied more time and energy in the history of human beings than the three F's: fighting, fucking, and filosophizing (the philosophy of transformation, magic), but to what end? They tend to be viewed with a strange apathy instead of being seen as an intrinsic part of humans Being. The Dark Arts of war, sex, and magic hold the key to the human soul.

There is a built in mechanism in each of us that propels us toward growth. Change is a natural part of everything in the universe. The highest realization for Man is the manifestation of an immortal soul. In order to attain this highest realization of Being, mankind must capitalize on our inherent strengths and nature.

Drawing on the findings of science, religion, sociology, psychology, philosophy, mythology, history, ancient texts, and metaphysics, *The Dark Arts of Immortality* explains how to harness and augment the energy of our innate drives. Through personal combat, sexual fantasy, and mystic rituals the death drive (mortido), sex drive (libido), and growth drive (physis) can provide doorways to supra-consciousness. These core altered states of being (fury, ecstasy, and exaltation) grant preternatural physical, mental, and spiritual abilities. The synthesis of these attributes will elevate personal power in this world and allow one to manifest a divine Being in the afterlife.

Mastering the 'Dark Arts' will bring you everything in this life you are willing to work toward. Just reading this work will empower you even without practicing the techniques. It will change how you see and interact with the universe. It will give you an understanding of human nature and the worlds we live in. It will awaken things you already know but forgot or don't consciously think about. It will give you some basic tools to change the You-Universe relationship thus automatically changing your mundane life. It will give you the methodology behind the Dark Arts and the secrets to their power. If you choose, however, to study and practice the Dark Arts of Immortality, your personal transformation will be nothing short of astounding.

Proceeding with a discussion of immortality and the important role the Dark Arts play requires a clear understanding of what we mean by immortality. There are various types of immortality and each has its own paradigm. There are thousands of religions and each one has its particular spin on the afterlife. Next, we need to have an understanding of the Universe and Man's relationship to it. Then we can move into a discussion of the Dark Arts and how they transcend traditional religions and cultures. Keep in mind the aim is receiving personal power now, not just in some elusive afterlife, while at the same time giving one's Self the greatest chance at immortality.

The chapters in the first section of the book (Preliminaries, Reality Check, Cycle of Interaction, and Left Hand Path) establish a modern outlook on the world at large and the context within which we all function. Much of the basic information may be familiar to you but it will also create a foundation of knowledge drawing upon some new findings in psychology and philosophy, and set the universal stage upon which war, sex, and magic interact with the individual. The next chapters (Divine Paradigm, Self-Evolution Theory, and Hidden Powers) reveal some of the secrets our ancestors passed on through oral legends, folklore, mythology, and runic texts. Being closer to nature and technologically less advanced gave them a unique outlook on the human spirit that needs to be understood by the modern warrior/lover/magician. The next sections contain the core teachings of the book. These chapters (The Art of War, The Art of Sex, and The Art of Magic) elaborate on the techniques necessary to implement the knowledge and secrets uncovered in the previous chapters. The powers obtained by the supra-conscious states of fury, ecstasy, and exaltation and the methods of attaining such states of being are covered in depth. The final chapters (Synergy and Conclusions) explain the concepts of synthesizing the benefits of these states of being and the elimination of the disadvantages. Some intermediate stages of undirected synthesis such as "Flow", "The Zone" and "Rapture" are discussed with the aim of not only explaining possible experiences obtained by the practitioner of the Dark Arts but also to prevent the mistake of stopping short of the goal. This last section also lists some suggestions for further study and organizations that can help.

At some point in life, nearly everyone feels powerless in today's society. People have been let down by traditional religious institutions, the government, and big business so consistently they don't trust anyone to take care of them. It is time to take charge of your own quest for personal power and immortality. I congratulate you on your courage. Beware though: the answers you find may be disturbing. Still, I commend you on your strong individuality. Be prepared, for you are about to find the answers you have long been seeking.

I. Preliminaries

*I write for a species of man
that does not yet exist:
for the "masters of the earth."*
                        -Friedrich Nietzsche

They say there is nothing new under the sun. They are right. Fortunately you have chosen to seek in the darkness, for it is in the darkness that all secrets are hidden. It is in the darkness that the unknown lies in wait. It is in the darkness that truth devours the known. It is in the darkness that all great quests must transpire. And it is in darkness where you will find your divine Self. Beware! For no man can delve into the darkest regions of the psyche and return unscathed. Yet only afterward is one truly ready to master one's own destiny.

The purpose of this book is to start you on the path to divine personal ascension. In other words, our goal is for you to receive the knowledge necessary to transform yourself into an immortal Being. Don't kid yourself, there is no guarantee you have an immortal spirit gifted to you at birth that is immutable. What you have is the potential to become a demigod but, just like many other possibilities in life, it can be squandered. Your body can be damaged or not fully develop due to genetic abnormalities or illness. Your mind can have similar difficulties, become damaged, or remain underdeveloped. Likewise, the spirit of a person runs the same risks. Just as your mind and body can atrophy due to disuse, so too can your spirit. The worst problem of all is wasted potential, and to me the potential most wasted is experience. In describing the author William James in the introduction to The Varieties of Religions Experience, Jacques Bazun says,

> "...he loved *experience* - the stuff of life as nearly "raw" as possible, before it has been worked on by the social conventions and kneaded into a common, palatable dough... he believed that the sinner is closer to god than the conventionally good man, because life is given us as a passion; it is, as Keats said, a vale of soul-making." (vii)

The title speaks clearly enough, this book is about immortality the soul seeks after as developed through the Dark Arts. For centuries we have lost touch with these secrets due to our fear of the darkness. It is time for the bold to embrace the shadows and to dance with the invisible. Every waking moment you are walking a sorrowful path toward death. You should ask yourself what you can and will do in the here and now to guarantee survival beyond the veil.

Barriers

Some of what is said in this work will be new to you. Some of it will resonate like thoughts from your own mind. There is a fine line between reality and fantasy, between truth and fiction. Each is needed for different reasons but it is up to the reader to figure out which is most necessary at any given time. The mind cannot always tell the difference. It is best to recognize such truths on your own in order to create the greatest benefits. Realize as well that in fantasy lies power and sometimes truth, but both impact you in their own way. It is like explaining an escalator to an aborigine. Although lacking a context within which to understand an escalator having never seen gears or motors, and having no concept of electricity, they will be changed none-the-less by a description of how one operates. Their mind will be expanded beyond its previous boundaries forever and opened to new vistas of creativity. It is also like a visual gestalt, such as one of those drawings that have a picture within a picture (i.e. a beautiful woman transposed over an ugly old hag). The visual image you see changes depending on how and where you focus your eyes. Upon first examination you may see only one image. If someone points out there is another possibility, you will search harder and find it for yourself resulting in a gain of insight and satisfaction. Upon subsequent viewings, it will be impossible for you not to see both truths.

Much of the knowledge in this work will go to waste if you do not experience it for yourself. The great thing about this material is that you have already experienced an altered state of higher consciousness. No one has to prove it to you, only clarify what it was you felt and help you understand how to capitalize on it. For example, if you are or have been involved in sports you probably experienced the "Zone" resulting in a near perfect athletic performance and a distorted sense of motion around you. As an artist, musician, or hobbyist you will have experienced "Flow" which is a state of bliss and time distortion brought on by the performance of your craft. Some people have even had this experience working on their car, cleaning house, or doing their job at work. And for those devout individuals involved in rituals, whether they are religious or magical in nature, have undoubtedly reached a sense of "Rapture". This is an intuitive feeling of power and being larger than one's self. It is also accompanied by a perceived time warping. Most people never learn why they had these bouts of altered consciousness, never learn to expand their powers, and never learn how to re-create them at will. The reasons why and the answers to how to control these experiences are in these pages.

It is a truism that nice guys finish last. That may be difficult for some people to believe because it has to be experienced for one's self, but for anyone who has lived it, it is a given which makes perfect sense. The Dark Arts of Immortality are that way as well. Most of the knowledge gained from them is in the practice. No amount of talking or reading can replace the practical work involved. It is like the vast difference between being told about fire, seeing fire for one's self, and being burned by fire. Gunter Figal points out in his work *For a Philosophy of Freedom and Strife*, "The most essential element in an art lies not in success, but in the fact that one understands the limitations of the craft, and in this way first liberates the craft. The art of recognition is the secret essence of every art" (194). I have liberated the Dark Arts from the dungeon of obscurity. It is up to you to do the work required to experience their essence.

Another major barrier to understanding is the weight given to scientific knowledge. We rely on science for many of our answers but that same understanding changes as new facts come to light. Currently much of reality is not accessible to the measuring instruments of the scientific method. This somehow causes doubt about the existence of a great portion of the Universe. Sometimes it even casts doubt on concepts it can't even quantify especially when reaching outside its own walls of objective reality. One encounters problems when trying to study across fields of science. There are so many gaps in scientific knowledge that Thoreau once pointed out that we *know* is an infinitely small amount when compared to what we *don't know*. We often abandon the hard won wisdom of primitive peoples because we mistakenly believe that since they do not have scientific facts to confirm their knowledge it is somehow less relevant or even worse, irrelevant.

Metaphysics

In their essay *The Metaphysics of the Matrix*[1], Jorge J. E. Garcia & Jonathan J. Sanford describe metaphysics this way,

> "Another way to distinguish metaphysics from the sciences, theology, and other areas of philosophy, and to establish what is involved in carrying out its task, is to say that metaphysics tries (1) to develop a list of the most general categories into which all other categories may be classified and (2) to establish how the less general categories are related to these. The task of metaphysics, then, is twofold: First, to develop a list of the most general categories and, second, to categorize everything else in terms of these. Obviously, to do this is precisely to try to develop the kind of overall, comprehensive view of the world in which both scientific and theological elements are included." (157)

One of the major difficulties in a work like this is the limited amount of space possible in a single book. A dozen volumes could not exhaust many of the topics here. Therefore, it was necessary to condense them to their essential values. I will not ask you to take anything on faith as if it is a higher form of understanding than reason, but there is not enough room to go into every topic at length. Some obstacles had to be jumped. P. D. Ouspensky points out the difficulty involved in understanding passing between areas of study in *Tertium Organum* by saying,

> "We fail to understand many things, because we specialize too easily and too drastically. Philosophy, religion, psychology, mathematics, natural sciences, sociology, history of culture, art - each has its own special literature. There is nothing embracing the whole in its entirety. Even the *bridges* between separate literatures are built badly and ineffectually, and are often altogether absent. This creation of special literatures is the chief evil and chief obstacle to right understanding of things. Each 'literature' evolves its own terminology, its own language, incomprehensible to representatives of other literatures and *not corresponding* to any of the other languages. In this way each one limits itself still more drastically, dissociates itself from the others and renders its frontiers impassable." (262)

---

[1] From *The Philosophy of the Matrix*.

So don't feel it is mandatory to be an expert in each of the fields touched on. With what you already know and what I have added here you should be perfectly capable of success. It is more important to practice the Dark Arts themselves, but if you want to fill in any gaps in your knowledge a basic reading list is included.

Disbelief and Discernment

There are many things in life that cannot be proven yet. Sometimes knowledge has to be drawn from experience, conjecture, and aesthetics. I use the word aesthetics here because at its core it is related to intuition, a form of direct knowledge (*noesis*). An attempt has been made to avoid some of the wild assumptions of other works in this field (especially those related to religion and magic). Rational and intuitive thought based on facts, experience, and similarities can certainly clear a way toward true knowledge and understanding (enlightenment).

For a moment it will be necessary to suspend disbelief, but not discernment. You already have practice suspending disbelief every time you watch TV and allow it to fiddle with your emotions as if the events were real. To get into the film you have to forget that it is just fake people, projected from light and celluloid onto a white canvass and from your current point of view there was originally cameramen, gaffers, grips, and directors.

Many of the topics covered here have an entire body of literature devoted to it. To gain clarity from the work at hand you will be required to bring bits and fragments from many sources and experiences and utilize a dash of intellectual conjecture. Some of it will be difficult for certain minds to understand or agree with. That is ok, as long as your critical eye can see the truths lying behind the concepts. I can only present the material so well. The rest, as they say, is up to you. I cannot force my opinions on you, nor correct your errors of interpretation, nor suggest you exclude your own insights. In fact, I am counting on them. You will latch onto some subjects and reject others. You will create your own masterpiece from the colorful pallet I set before you.

The foundation of this knowledge is sound but starting this work from a standpoint of disbelief will keep that knowledge hidden from you until another time.

Germanic Format

It would be impossible to include every culture and religion in a work of this sort. One branch of Indo-European culture is called the Germanic (which includes such cultures as the Gothic, French, Norse, Scandinavian, English, etc.). Due to the rich heritage of the Germanic peoples, and my fluency with Germanic culture, folklore, and mythology, I chose to make them the focal point of the concepts presented hereafter. The myths, legends, and literature of many other cultures (Oriental, Egyptian, African, etc.) could be substituted and still validate the core truths of the Dark Arts of Immortality.

Visions

There are times when an inner voice speaks to us. When we are children, we listen and interact with that voice in a playful wonderful innocence. As we grow older we start to ignore it because we are too busy or too "grown up." This inner voice often reacts by becoming merely a critic, and sadly one we often grant entirely too much power over our lives. Dudley Young identifies the proper perspective our ancestors already knew when he writes in *Origins of the Sacred* "...the adult task is not to abandon one's infantile desires but to so clothe and transform them through art and religion that they may again be housed, and paradise perhaps regained, in such a way that life is lived *more* abundantly..." (pg112).

First Darkness

Hariison: "Odin..."

Hariison: "Odin..."

Hariison: "Awaken Allfather. I have come a long way."

Odin: "Why have you come?"

Hariison: "I have searched a long time."

Odin: "WHY have you come?"

Hariison: "I need answers."

Odin: "To what questions?"

Hariison: "All of them."

Odin: "And what are you willing to give."

Hariison: "Anything that is mine to give."

Odin: "How much do you know?"

Hariison: "Less than some, but more than most."

Odin: "You have done well."

Hariison: "Then my search is over?"

Odin: "No. It is only now that it can begin."

Definitions

Will- The power of choosing; the faculty or endowment of the spirit by which it is capable of choosing.

Belief- Any cognitive content held as true.

Augment- To make (something already developed or well under way) greater, as in size, extent, or quality.

Violate- To break or disregard laws or rules.

Causality- The principle of, or relationship between, cause and effect.

Intent- The state of one's mind (in regard to an anticipated outcome) at the time one carries out an action.

Magic- A methodology whereby the will, guided by belief, augments or violates causality in accordance with one's intent.

Pneuma - soul or spirit

Pneumatology - the study of spiritual beings or phenomena.

Noujective – the inner spiritual world of Wo/Man.

Disclaimer

One of the most intriguing lines in *The Devil's Notebook* by Anton Szandor LaVey is "The lack of imagination and staying power of the occult movement is showing through the veneer of the incompetents who fill its ranks." (29). This is intriguing, because at first it offends certain sensibilities; especially since most people who come to the occult world feel there is something essentially wrong with the rest of society, and they are right. Yet after some thought it becomes blatantly clear how true his statement is. The people who come to the underworld in search of answers are no more likely to act on that knowledge than someone reading it out of pure curiosity is. In fact, they are probably less likely because just by joining they think they are actually doing something.

Action is the key to success. We are beings of the material dimension where action has the greatest power and influence. Yet, it is the power we tend to consciously use least often. If you are a couch potato and think that reading this book is actually going to dramatically change your life, you are mistaken. The occult world is full of these fantasy elitists who never practice anything other than reading and criticizing. To separate yourself from the herd of humanity you must come to the darkness AND act.

Practicing the Dark Arts is hard work. Probably the hardest work you will ever do. You must be mentally, physically, and spiritually prepared. If you are out of shape put this book down right now and do 10 push-ups, then go out and walk or jog two miles. When you return write down an exercise schedule and consult with a physician. If you don't have the discipline to take care of your personal grooming and health, there is no way you will be able to complete the work of the Dark Arts of Immortality. After you have completed these preliminary steps it will be ok to read the book and, after you are in shape, to practice its contents. If you are already in shape and have had some other successes in the real world (i.e. education, work) then by all means please continue. You are truly elite, and way ahead of the curve. If you have also been on the quest for a while now, I am glad you have chosen this book because you will be well rewarded. The techniques of the Dark Arts are the answers you were looking for. By elevating consciousness and being you may find a solution to physical immortality. At the minimum, you will overcome time and entropic forces and transform yourself into a Divinely Ascended Immortal Soul.

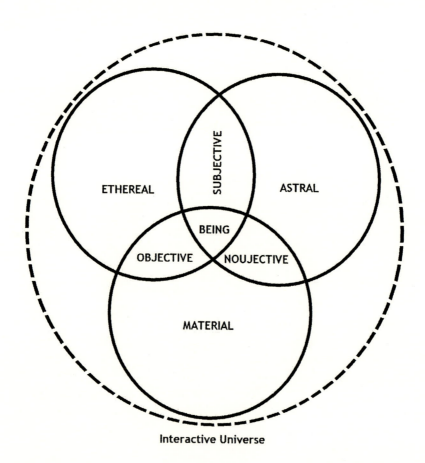
Interactive Universe

II. Reality Check

*From the point of view of ordinary language,
the further reaches of both nature and spirit
lie in the domain of the in-expressible.*
- HUSTON SMITH

In order to proceed with a discussion of immortality and the important role the Dark Arts play in its attainment, we must first understand what we mean by immortality. There are various types of immortality and each has its own unique paradigm. There are thousands of religions and each one has its particular beliefs concerning the afterlife. Next, we will need to have an understanding of the universe and Man's relationship to it. Then when we move into a discussion of the Dark Arts of Immortality it will be clear how they transcend all religions and cultures to arrive at the root of Man's need. There is no other method that provides better scientific and theological balance for achieving personal immortality as well as providing a more profound existence here and progress for the species in general. As with many things however it will not come easy. Many of you will fall by the wayside.

Everything that enters the conscious mind (even things we are not fully aware of) passes into the subconscious. Events act similarly in that they occur in the present then pass into the past. Just as current events are a result of things that have built up in the past, so too are our conscious thoughts built upon not only our past experiences (we are aware of) but also the collective memories in our subconscious. Our brain has become a huge neural construct of belief. Howard Bloom explains part of the difficulty inherent in any type of rebellion against the ideals and habits you have held for most of your life in *The Lucifer Principle* by saying,

> "It's easy to see why humans are willing to fight to the death to defend the memes [self-replicating cultural ideas] that constitute their belief systems. To allow a faith or ideology to be overthrown would be to abandon a massive neural fabric into which you've invested an entire life, a network that cannot easily be replaced, perhaps that cannot be replaced at all." (138)

Aim of Religion

Religion, as it has become to be accepted, is a method of control taking its place alongside of legislation and economics. Currently nearly every aspect of a person's life is an exercise in control by some group or another. Big business controls the standard of living and monopolizes most peoples waking hours. The government controls freedom of action through laws, the military, and taxation, all the while giving the illusion of guaranteeing freedom. The church sets the standard for moral and ethical practices, which are used to keep men passive and dependent. The church has wedged itself between Man, his spirit and his gods by convincing him that they hold the keys to the invisible world and Man is not strong enough, nor smart enough, to enter it by himself.

Make no mistake; the church (like government and business) is an institution of men not of God. Prior to such things as nationalism and economics, religion was a spiritual technology used to help Man deal with mortality and understand his place in the universe. It was an attempt to get in touch with the spirit, a part of Man he felt but of which he was unsure. It was not a set of laws imposed from the top down but a flowering of a Man's nature toward the divine. Its primary goal was to point towards Man's immortality.

Man has spent centuries under this control. It takes an effort of superhuman will to break free of such restraints. But first it requires extraordinary awakening to even realize the predicament. You may have to start small and work your way up to bigger and bigger issues. The easiest way to begin is by becoming self-reliant. Stop paying someone else to fix every problem in your life. It could be as little as replacing a sink in your bathroom instead of calling a contractor, or as confusing as doing your own divorce instead of hiring a lawyer (easier than you think). The bottom line is that the more you do this the more you will learn you don't need their proof of power. You can do it for yourself. It will do you more good than you can imagine right now but just try it and see.

It is time to set the record straight. If you boil all religions down to their foundation you will find this one underlying principle. The true aim of religion for Man is personal immortality. People want to know there is life after death and how they are to attain it. They have wrongly believed it was going to be handed to them by the church. They think that only through the church can they find this elusive invisible power. They are in good hands so to speak. They trust in an institution of men, but that trust has been betrayed. Many people have started looking to ancient cultures and writings for some sense of the truth. They realize most current institutions run by men are corrupt. As such they can be of no real assistance to the individual in regards to his personal benefit. It is time to go back to Man's origins and find what he seeks within himself. William James puts it thusly,

> "One may say truly, I think, that personal religious experience has its root and center in mystical states of consciousness; so for us, who in these lectures are treating personal experience as the exclusive subject of our study, such states of consciousness ought to form the vital chapter from which the other chapters get their light." (318)

Types of Immortality

There are several different beliefs regarding immortality that have been passed on in different cultures and in different ages. I will touch briefly on some of them but focus my attention on two. One thing that stands out clearly through them all is Man has always believed in spirit. It probably started in times of great stress when he detected a nature within himself he could not quite identify. It could have been anger over an offense, excitement over a mate, or wonder at a waterfall. Primitive or modern we still have those same energies that intensify our mundane existence. Man has always had power within himself and the stories of heroes who utilized it have been repeated for centuries. The power is not in some hypothetical future, but right now. It is already within and has been all along. We are heirs to a divine heritage just waiting to be enacted.

In a physical sense, consider the ramifications of all the actions you take during your life upon the world. You are sending out ripples of cause and effect billions of years into the future, possibly to infinity. This means that each act someone performs can eventually affect all other people in the entire world. Everyone's very existence affects the universe forever. Children are another type of material immortality. A physical manifestation of you survives as long as you bear progeny. Their actions compound the affect you have on the world. The last form of physical immortality would be eternal bodily survival here without death. Not many cultures hold this belief for long, but it has been a passing quest throughout all ages (i.e. the fountain of youth).

In a mental sense there are the teachings left in the minds of others when we die. We could be talking about individuals known during our lifetimes, the thoughts we put in writing, or simply the memory of deeds done. In Western cultures there are also theories that memories can be passed on genetically in some form, while in Eastern cultures there is a belief in a connection with an akashic record (a warehouse of thoughts everyone can access). A ghostly continuation of mind would fit neatly into this category as well.

Spiritual immortality is still believed by many cultures and in many different aspects as well. It is possible that after death of the body the spirit is reborn in another body to live again. Reincarnation of this type is very popular, especially in Eastern thought. In Western thought, there is a form of reincarnation whereby rebirth is created by modeling one's life after someone else (usually an ancestor). This is one of the ideas we will elaborate on later. There is the concept of a movement of consciousness in connection with spirit to another dimension. That movement could culminate in an afterlife of some sort (Heaven, Hel, Elysian Fields) or in a merging of consciousness with some cosmic aspect (Nirvana, God). It is clear in classical religious philosophy the traditional afterlife involves merging with God. The study of philosophers of all modern religions will point to this union of Self with God.

There is of course another option. I am speaking of the complete transformation of the enlightened Self into a Divinely Ascended Immortal Soul. That is Man's divine destiny and the other form of immortality we will be expanding upon in this work.

Soul Immortality

The aim of this book is to guide people on the path toward Awakening and Self-realization. Nothing less than the evolution into a higher state of Being so that crossing the threshold of death will be a step toward Self deification. A reading of the most ancient texts show how old and universal this goal is. The entire history of man has been the race for this beckoning object. Our entire Being is suffused with the energy and drive necessary to perpetuate and augment our consciousness and personal identity.

The benefits of this work will also develop a person here in this life, allowing for the advancement of the human race. We are not going to deny our natural desires and tendencies. We are just going to harness that energy and direct it more consciously and conscientiously. This life is absolutely necessary for any growth to take place. The clues have been passed down to us over and over since the beginning of recorded history. Some lie right in plain view but go unnoticed or they have been rejected due to moral confusion and forgetfulness. Dudley Young points the way,

> "The myths that compose the religious and political structure of every culture are tales of power, how it is to be found and where it is to be used... we must put ourselves back to school with our forebears,

to recall the myths that legitimize our existence and tell us how to live with godly power." (27)

So now we have an idea where to find the answers. The questions that remain are then what are we looking for and what will we find there? The answer is 'godly power' in the form of fury, ecstasy, and exaltation. In *The Morning of the Magicians*, Louis Pauwels & Jacques Bergier conclude by saying "Let us stick to the facts. The phenomenon of the super-conscious state can be attributed to the existence of an immortal soul. This notion has been advanced for thousands of years without ever having done much toward solving the problem." (354). The time has come to 'solve the problem' as it were and put the knowledge of altered states of consciousness to work for us.

We have become spiritual sheep in more ways than one. We must realize that our immortality is our responsibility. The lethargy infecting us must be cured. We have lost our perspective on spirit. We no longer see ourselves as sacred. We no longer see human life as sacred. We no longer see the world as sacred ground. The problem is grim indeed. We personify animals to the point of spending more time and money protecting their rights than we do homeless and destitute homo-sapiens. We elevate animal life and marginalize human life. Yet we are the beings that have the potential to conquer death by Becoming.

Self-immortality is the primary goal. Within the Germanic framework that immortality is defined in two ways: endless existence and enduring fame. We can secure infinite continuation of our current identity, and leave an indelible mark on the physical world, which will reverberate throughout eternity. Humans in the Germanic cosmology who ascend to immortal status are called Einherjar (male) or Valkyrie (female). These warriors reside in the halls of the Gods (Valhalla and Folkvangr) until Ragnarok, when they will fight for the future of all humanity. By becoming paragons upon this warriors' path we create the desire to follow us in those individuals who would emulate our deeds, thereby not just continuing our impact in all worlds but also helping ensure victory at Ragnarok. We also attain more power in this physical life by learning and growing from the experience. Our Being here will change as we attempt to transform and metamorphose our soul.

Nature of the Universe

The Germanic worldview consists of nine worlds; ironically consistent with our nine planets considering they evolved this belief thousands of years before the discovery of other planets. An important aspect of this cosmology is the belief the universe is divided into three levels (dimensions): Upper/Middle/Lower. This is reflected in other cultures with Macro/Meso/Micro, Heaven/Earth/Underworld, etc.

Later chapters will build upon the explanation of the use of Universe but this section will serve as an initial frame of reference. The term Universe will be used to refer to All-That-Is/Is Not. The concept of "All-That-Is" is a pretty obvious one, but what is meant by "Is-Not?" There are things that have not manifested in our reality yet, but that does not mean they do not exist for the Universe. Since the Universe includes the potential for all things, and time is not necessarily a law It operates under, we can say It also includes all that Is-Not *yet*. Heraclitus taught that the Universe was ruled by strife. That even at the smallest level there was constant movement and change if we could only see it. This concept was born from a man millennia ago and is still proving itself through physicists even today.

The Universe is divided into three dimensions: the Material Dimension, Astral Dimension, and Ethereal Dimension. The dimensions overlay each other so effects in one affect the others and by extension the Universe. Fred Alan Wolf in *Parallel Universes* explains how science is still adjusting its own understanding,

> "The fact that the future may play a role in the present is a new prediction of the mathematical laws of quantum physics. If interpreted literally, the mathematical formulas indicate not only how the future enters our present but also how our minds may be able to "sense" the presence of parallel universes [dimensions]." (23)

Since the term Universe encompasses everything it cannot be beside itself. We will need to separate this concept by using 'parallel dimensions' instead, which is what he and the rest of the scientific community are really talking about anyway. These three dimensions (Material, Astral, and Ethereal) are filled with the worlds of Man: Objective worlds, Subjective worlds, and Noujective worlds respectively. Noujective is a term created for this work and is a bastardization of pneuma (meaning spirit), nouminal (known to exist but not experienced), and numinous (meaning supernatural mysterious, holy). These refer to Man's place in the Universe, and we will return to this concept later. Suffice it to say the objective world of Man is of the body and involves the things he interacts with, the subjective world is of the mind and the thoughts he utilizes and the noujective is of the spirit and is detected on rare occasions through intuition and emotion.

The Material dimension is home to the body and consists of all physical phenomena (fire, electricity, planets, etc.). It is the dimension most closely understood because people experience it every day and it appears to be the root of Man's existence. Hence, it should be the dimension most likely to yield up its secrets. In order for that to happen we have to know how to act in it and how to evaluate our results. Many mysteries are to be solved by examining the writing on the walls of material reality and it is likely that the other dimensions have similar signposts just waiting for our discovery. We shall see soon enough.

All Objective worlds exist within this Material dimension. To put its size and scope into perspective consider the following. It takes 11 days to count to one million counting at a rate of one number per second. At that same rate it would take 32 years to count to one billion. Our solar system (one of over 300 billion in the Milky Way galaxy) is over 7 billion miles across. If it were shrunk down to the size of a tennis ball, by an equal scale the Milky Way galaxy (480 million billion miles across) would be larger than the United States of America. The age of the galaxy (one of over a hundred billion in the Material dimension) is estimated at 12 billion years with the age of the earth estimated at 4.5 billion years and there are billions of planets billions of years older in this galaxy alone.

The Astral dimension is the landscape of thought. All subjective worlds of Man exist in the astral dimension. The human mind can encompass the entire Material dimension. (You just did it while I was describing it to you. You saw the stars, planets, nebulae, etc. in your minds eye at the same time you were reading the words.) There are as many different subjective worlds as there are intelligent life forms in the Material dimension. The Astral dimension is at least as large as the Material and possibly much larger. When you consider that this one planet in the Material dimension houses 5 billion subjective worlds creating thoughts every second of every day (even while sleeping), it is quite possible that the Astral dimension dwarfs the Material by comparison (even without assuming that other worlds hold intelligent life in the abundance this one does). One thing is clear, there is a difference in kind from Man's body (objective) and mind (subjective). *Smith* concurs,

> "The theoretical argument asks if matter can ever account for sentience, or mind in the widest sense of the word. This is a timeworn issue, of course, one of the thorniest in the entire history of philosophy. What we can say briefly is that no convincing materialistic explanation of mind has been forthcoming. Matter is located in space; one can specify precisely where a given tree, let us say, resides. But if one asks where his perception of the tree is located he can expect difficulties. The difficulties increase if he asks how tall his perception of the tree is; not how tall is the tree he sees, but how tall his seeing of it." (67).

He goes on to say, "A final line of argument is empirical. Instead of arguing that mind is a distinctive kind of entity, it argues that it functions in distinctive ways. It plays by different rules, conforms to laws that differ in kind from those that matter exemplifies." (68).

The Ethereal dimension is the abode of the unknown and the mark of the divine and is therefore the least understandable. It is impossible to *know* anything about the Ethereal dimension directly (other than knowing it is not known) but you can on occasion *feel* it intuitively. Physical sciences (Biology, Chemistry, Physics, etc.) can detect and quantify the Material dimension just as the conceptual sciences (Psychology, Mathematics, and Philosophy) can ascertain certain aspects of the Astral. Just because these sciences can't prove something exists does not mean it does not. They can only work within the fields of the Material and Astral dimensions. Obviously they still don't completely understand consciousness (although they can map some brain functions). Although science has indicators that point to the Ethereal dimension it lies just out of reach because it is different in kind from the Material and Astral dimensions in the same ways that spirit is different from body and mind. Dudley Young explains the confusion this way "...the simple world of predictable stresses and strains that Newton invited us to live in now seems to be an illusion we sensibly adopt in order to stay sane, but underneath it all the woodwork is crawling with unpredictability..." (35). It is this unpredictability that is explained by the idea of these parallel dimensions that make up the whole of the Universe. Particles that disappear completely and have other paradoxical properties, seemingly impossible in the Material dimension, are quite at home within the broader confines of an Astral and Ethereal dimension. Some current ideas among physicists such as String Theory, Supersymmetry and Dark Matter are used to explain the behavior of the smallest particles and all hint at an Ethereal dimension. Houston Smith adds,

> "This shift [in sciences knowing process] occurs when the physicist comes upon the very large and fast in nature, or conversely the very small... It is customary to describe this situation by saying that nature in these reaches is 'counterintuitive,' meaning that it disregards and violates - transcends - the categories of space and time as we intuit them.... (1) the fact that nature at its edges performs in ways that differ in kind from the way it meets our senses, and (2) the fact that our imaginations have nothing to build with save the building blocks our senses provide - and we arrive at the point the phrase 'counterintuitive' was coined to make. In its further reaches the physical universe [Material dimension] dons forms and functions

we cannot visualize, in imagination any more than with the eyes in our heads. There is no way in which we can image them." (104-105)

Thus far there is no mind particle to point to, and since it cannot be explained by the Astral dimension alone, we are again guided to the Ethereal as a welcomed solution.

Could we assume that the ethereal dimension is equal in size to either of the others? This would make complete sense if each particle in the Material dimension winked into and out of the Astral and Ethereal, the three dimensions phasing together in some as yet incomprehensible way, to make up the Universe. However, let us also consider the typical subjective world that consists of thoughts, ideas, and imaginings. Now how much exists as potential that is hidden from us, things we don't know compared to what we do and have not even conceived. Don't confuse "hidden" in the ethereal sense from simply the things we don't know about the Material dimension. We could make a logical conclusion the Ethereal dimension may surpass the Astral by a scale equal to that dimension's vastness over the Material. When we discover some new fact, it seems to lead to dozens of unanswerable questions. This gives rise to theories conjecturing the more knowledge we gain, the more we discover we don't know. So it could be that the potential of the Ethereal grows exponentially as we try to understand it. The Ethereal is different in kind from the Astral and Material dimensions.

	Universe	
Material Dimension	Astral Dimension	Ethereal Dimension
Objective World	Subjective World	Noujective World
	Man	

Nature of Man

Now it is time to place Man within the Universe, the microcosm within the Macrocosm. There is an old proverb that says no man can enter the same river twice because it is never the same river nor the same man. The implication is that Man is constantly changing just like the Universe. As L. Ron Hubbard put it in *Scientology: The Fundamentals of Thought* "Man or any life form in this universe seems to love problems... Problems keep up interest... The insanity among the idle is a matter of problem scarcity." (40). So it appears that "strife" is as much in the nature of Man as it is the Universe.

In every culture around the world it has been accepted that Man is of body, mind and spirit. There are disagreements on the nature of these three elements, of course, but they are fairly well universal. Most people would accept body and mind because they are directly experienced. If they argue against spirit, then what is the point of discussing immortality or the need for religion in the first place. The qualities of mind alone are not sufficient to support it. Further delineation of Man and his experience of the Universe will show three worlds of man, the Objective World, Subjective World, and Noujective World (remember pneuma, nouminal, and numinous). These words originated because humans can sense and intuit spirit. As Pauwels and Bergier point out in *The Morning of the Magicians*,

> "What is essential is to know whether Man possesses in unexplored regions of his being, superior instruments, enormous amplifiers, as it were, of his intelligence - a whole equipment to enable him to conquer and comprehend the Universe, to conquer and comprehend himself, and to shoulder his whole destiny." (353)

And if we wish to seek these "instruments" out we have to look no further than ourselves.

Distinguishing between the three worlds of Man is easy. The Objective (material) world of a man is just that, the world of physical objects he interacts with. It is his immediate surroundings and is filled with things like cars, buildings, people, and rocks. The Subjective world of a man is the way he thinks about himself and those objects. It is the mental arena of thoughts and beliefs and includes his entire psyche. The Noujective world of man is much harder to nail down, but is simply put the awareness of his own spirit and the communications it sometimes provides him (most often through emotion, intuition, and drives). It relates to the dimension of the divine and the hidden.

Think of man almost like a wormhole through the dimensions (consider the light at the end of the tunnel visions people have during near death experiences), and a gateway from the Material world to the others. We have to get away from the human tendency to make everything either or. Things don't always fit into neat little categories. Since strife is so prevalent in the Universe it only makes sense that things change, even the nature of things change (except change). Everything is in flux depending on how you view it. Man (consciousness) resides in the material world but (consciousness) touches the other worlds as well. Man's body is material but his consciousness is immaterial, a duality that causes much confusion even before questioning emotional issues.

Each of these worlds is constantly undergoing change and manifestation. Obviously these three worlds correlate to the dimensions. As such, if something (anything) in man lies outside of the Material and Astral dimensions then spirit must exist. The aspects of Man manifest in the material through action, from the astral through speech, and from the ethereal through will. And since we are so strongly rooted in the Material dimension, it would seem obvious to utilize the body's activities in the objective world to seek empowerment. It is also the best starting point for forays into the other dimensions for the purpose of Self-discovery.

The worlds overlap and interact. Within the self this is much easier to see. We get direct feedback from actions that affect the Objective world, thereby affecting our Subjective world, and the Noujective world. Within the Material dimension, the Objective worlds of men lie next to each other affecting each through causal relationships or by direct interaction. Since we look for patterns to lead us to answers about other areas, it is safe to assume the Astral world is composed of Subjective worlds that reside in some relation to each other as well. However, they also communicate through mediums in the Material dimension (speech, writing, etc.). It is possible that another person's Subjective world sends ripples through the Astral dimension affecting us indirectly. Likewise for the Noujective world and Ethereal dimension it is possible to have contact through emotional contagion (although this would probably go entirely unnoticed by the conscious mind, and as discussed later the immensity may lessen the likelihood). However our Noujective world is less easy to clearly identify. For now, suffice it to say the form of knowing it presents is intuition, and the manifestation of will it produces is through the drives (which will be discussed later).

Being and Consciousness

The level of development and interaction one has with the three worlds affect one's Being in those worlds. We are by our very nature, social creatures. We are always involved in a context that includes other people and things. We can never detach ourselves from the world in its entirety nor avoid other human interaction completely. Different types of consciousness affect the type of Being we exhibit. In fact, as we will see later in the section on perception, Being can be improved by working on any area of the cycle of interaction with the Universe (perception, processing, or providing) but will be at its most powerful when all areas work in concert. Herein lies the problem. Most people believe themselves to be living somewhat optimally. They ascribe to themselves certain qualities they think they have but in no way do they really have any control over those characteristics. For example if you consider for a moment just your own thoughts. Try to sit perfectly still for one minute and focus on one concept or idea to the exclusion of all others. Go ahead. Ok, now how long did you make it before other thoughts pushed their way into your awareness or your mind wandered onto other subjects?

It is misleading and delusional for us to believe we have even a modicum of control over our own minds. So it is with consciousness that we must acquire capacities we think we already have but which, in fact, we are lacking (i.e. wakefulness, centeredness, unity, etc.).

In order to transform our Being-ness, we must first transform our consciousness. We must know where we are and where we want to go. In order to do that we have to understand the Universe, and ourselves then make a choice of what we want. This line of thinking will lead us right into the Dark Arts of Immortality.Being-ness is changing every moment whether we are aware of it or not. It may not be changing for the better, thus the necessity of understanding and gaining awareness of our Being. We will call this Awakening. Awakening will be the prerequisite to Ascending, which we will define as a change in the state of Being. The need for Awakening implies that we are currently asleep with our eyes open. Of the entire spectrum of light only a small band is normally visible to us. Much of light exists without our awareness. Similarly, much of the material world is in darkness with respect to our ability to perceive it. Consciousness and Being-ness are like that as well, hidden in the darkness away from our awareness. A lot of what goes on with our own body, mind, and spirit is normally not available to us. We must find the tools to bring these elements into our awareness and under our control. We must seek it out by admitting our deficiency and then gaining the abilities and powers we thought we already had.

During an experiment of the religious uses of hallucinogens, William James said,

> "One conclusion was forced upon my mind at that time, and my impression of its truth has ever since remained unshaken. It is that our normal waking consciousness, rational consciousness as we call it, is but one special type of consciousness, whilst all about it, parted from it by the filmiest of screens, there lie potential forms of consciousness entirely different...No account of the universe in its totality can be final which leaves these other forms of consciousness quite disregarded." (325)

He is quite right, but the methods he used to come to this realization will not fulfill our needs. We are grateful for his conclusion, but we need more information to guide us to discovery. In my theological, philosophical, and magical studies it seems to me there is a trend towards over-reliance upon meditation as tool to furthering oneself in such self-discovery and empowerment. If we are trying to find a higher form of consciousness should we not want to move consciousness away from sleep? We constantly use the metaphor of awakening. Why select a method like meditation that is closer to the unconscious state. Pauwels and Bergier hit the mark with the following:

> "It is not a question of a different level, but of a different speed. The same applies to the greatest mystics. The miracles, in nuclear physics as well as in psychology, are to be found in acceleration. And it is from this standpoint, we believe, that the third state of consciousness, the "awakened" state, should be studied... And yet, if such a state... is, in fact, a part of the equipment of our brain and body - could not this equipment, once it starts functioning, affect faculties in us other than our intelligence? If the "awakened" state is a property of some higher nervous system, this activation should be capable of affecting the whole body and endowing it with strange powers." (369)

The Dark Arts of Immortality will prove them right because they represent a complete system of repeatable and verifiable methodologies for attaining and synthesizing a supra-conscious state. As I mentioned earlier you have already experienced some form of this effect (the Zone, Flow, Rapture). The best way to get the mind revved up is to get the body revved up. It is through the body that we must work on consciousness. In this regard Edred Thorsson agrees by stating in *Runelore*,

> "The "substances" of the body are gateways to other aspects of the self, and they are the ultimate receptacles of magical work. Therefore, certain subtle substances in the body become focal points for the development of the self or the person of whole consciousness, aware of all aspects in an exalted ego state." (168)

Time and Entropy

Personal immortality will only be obtained by overcoming the laws of time and entropy. Our only direct experience of both is through altered states of consciousness, especially those of the supra-conscious variety. We are speaking, of course, of peak performance, optimal experience, and hyper emotion (the Zone, Flow, and Rapture respectively) and their core building blocks fury, ecstasy, and exaltation. We realize they create the conditions we need. As such we perceive time differently and also seem to experience energy of a nature not normally tapped, or at any rate a reversal of energy flow. We could say that states of consciousness change perception of the natural laws of time and the altered state of Being-ness changes the natural laws of entropy. Nietzsche characterizes it this way "Principle: There is an element of decay in everything that characterizes modern man: but close beside this sickness stand signs of an untested force and powerfulness of the soul." (68). It is time for us to test this force.

In our quest for immortality we must look to these two main elements affecting human life. Entropy is sometimes used to represent the natural tendency for a system to run down, decay, or exhaust its energy. It is also used in the context of energy not normally available for work. We must find a way to control both, but for now we will be seeking that energy not normally available. For human beings, time is an essential perception of the ego. Everything proceeds from something else in a linear fashion. We see things in terms of past, present, and future. For mathematicians and physicists, time is inseparable from space or distance. So the true essence of time is inexpressible. It is another instance of a concept or language barrier that cannot easily be crossed. Even our scientists have trouble explaining time in a way everyone can understand. We currently do not have a complete understanding of time, so we are confined to finding new ways in which to gain that knowledge. With each new experience of time distortion, though, you will begin to understand subtle nuances, here-to-fore, unrealized. A picture will start to emerge.

The first step is to be able to perceive time in more ways so new properties may be discovered or at least new ways of describing them. In *The Sweet Spot in Time*, John Jerome talks about the everyday training that certain artists undergo as part of their work that helps them see time differently:

> "I tap my foot to music and think I'm on the beat; any real musician can demonstrate convincingly that I'm not... Within that span of microseconds lies room I never dreamed existed, room wherein the good performer can place the note, the beat - or the movement - with delicate, deliberate control. In those microseconds there is room for performing art." (20)

This also applies to athletes who practice seeing fast moving objects like a 100 mile an hour pitch in baseball. To the rest of us, there would be no clear tracking of the ball. It would be a blur. This intentional practice of perceiving quickly is a sharp contrast to the stress response. Under highly stressful conditions the mind works at amazing speeds which also create a shift in the perception of time. This is an example of a higher state of consciousness inducing a distortion of time. Both of these areas of concern, the learned and the responsive, are necessary to our work. Learning to pay attention to time like the musician is easier than inducing the heightened state, but it is the latter that concerns us most here because of the additional benefits gained.

The supra-conscious states of the Dark Arts contain just this kind of time distortion as well. The three main supra-conscious states of being are fury, ecstasy, and exaltation. Each of these results in a distortion of time but has an added benefit of increasing certain human capabilities. Don Webb believes we have the potential to become gods and one of the steps in that process, as revealed in *Uncle Setnakt's Guide to the Left Hand Path*, he states thusly,

> "We have all had those moments of power, of knowing that we are alive, and that the world is meaningful. They are rare moments and usually we attribute them to an external trigger, perhaps even a mysterious or divine source. When we discover that we can have those moments *at will*, then we have begun the lifelong task of Rulership of the Inner World." (4)

Utilizing human drives to power states of being and consciousness is a method of ruling entropy. You harness biological power to enhance mental and spiritual being. The practice of magic does the same thing. People don't usually use the will in normal actions or speech. Training this way helps bring the will to bear on all activities (another lesson in resisting entropy). From the increase in normal human attributes, it is apparent there is a harnessing of energy normally not available. The primary forces behind these states are the human death, sex, and growth drives (Mortido, Libido, and Physis). So we have satisfied both conditions with the Dark Arts of Immortality: a new interaction with time and entropy.

Another element to consider in this section is the nature of our growth as beings. We are not isolated figures in the world. We are in a context wherein both time and entropy interact with Being. The ideas of karma and dharma are familiar to most people although they are frequently used incorrectly (the first is related to cycles of lifetimes, the second regarding effects within a single lifetime). Similar words are orlog and wyrd, which carry a richer meaning to the concept of time. They refer to the pattern of deeds and behavior that push certain choices and events in the future. They have a historical connection to heritage and fate. The Germanic cultural divisions of time and of the self, and their mingling, will be addressed more fully in a later chapter.

Creation and Evolution

There is a long running debate between theologians and scientists over the origin of Man and the earth. Religion claims a Divine Being created them both and scientists posit a theory of evolution (unconscious cause and effect) starting from the big bang. Yet what do we mean by evolution? Typically it is thought of in the classical Darwinian sense of 'survival of the fittest'. As we shall see later, that is not necessarily the right interpretation. P. D. Ouspensky states, in *The Psychology of Man's Possible Evolution*, that natural selection only develops us so far, and that to reach beyond that we must take matters into our own hands,

> "Then we must understand that *all men* cannot develop and become different beings. Evolution is the question of personal efforts, and in relation to the mass of humanity evolution is the rare exception. It may sound strange, but we must realize that it is not only rare, *but is becoming more and more rare.*" (8)

It is obvious most people will not be willing to put for the effort necessary.

Later, when we examine some of the social and cultural structures of humanity (genes, memes, and esses) to see how they reflect the nature of Man, we will see evidence of what Howard Bloom says here in *The Lucifer Principle*.,

> "Evolution is not just a competition between individuals. It is a competition between networks, between webs, between group souls. The new forms evolving on the face of this planet are not resident only in the features of individual animals or men. They don't merely consist of longer legs or bigger brains. The new forms are impalpable and invisible." (144)

So even for the definition of evolution itself there is probably some middle ground that will need to be decided on in order to have a consistent understanding of the term and its relation to creationism.

As with many questions in life the truth probably falls somewhere in between evolution and creation. That is the belief expressed in Germanic cosmogony. Out of the magically charged space of the Universe the first intelligent life emerged. The birth of the God Odin was soon to follow. With the powers he wielded he carved out existence and created the earth (Material dimension). With the aid of others he created man and woman (Objective,

Subjective, and Noujective worlds) and with the exception of one series of interventions, they were left to their own devices. In fact, in many stories the Gods/esses adventure among men and take them as companions in order to learn from them, and why not? Man's growth has been amazing.

In any case, the earth spins at about 1000 miles per hour and flies through space at about 58,000 miles per hour. Its age is estimated at 4.5 billion years old. Does it really matter, for Man, which is the truth (creation or evolution)? We can think of it this way. If we evolved as we are, then to continue improving we must look at our nature and expand upon it. On the other hand if we were created by some higher power (not unlikely considering the size, scope, and age of the physical dimension alone) then again our nature must be in line with that power's desires. It would be in our best interest to expand upon what we have been given. If neither of these are the case then we should still want the best possible development for ourselves, maybe even more so. So we come to only one viable solution: develop our intrinsic nature to the fullest of our potential.

The history of Man has not been a straight linear progression. There are fits and stops and great leaps forward. Barbara Ehrenreich describes one of the leaps in *Blood Rites: Origins and History of the Passions of War* like this,

> "The great advance in human evolution, the transition from the status of prey to that of predator, must have been, at some level, an act of transgression - a rebellion against the predator beast. It took enormous courage and defiance of our clawless, blunt-toothed, hominid ancestors to in any way challenge the beast's dominion. And insofar as the predator may also have been a provider and perhaps a kind of deity, the human rebellion against it surely ranks with Lucifer's uprising against heaven - the difference being that humans won... The myths of many cultures seem to recall this rebellion as a discrete and singular event, often the slaying of a fantastic beast by a male hero/god... In reality, of course, there could have been no single, decisive victory, and certainly not one achieved by a single, miraculously gifted individual. If these heroic myths tell us anything, it is that, on the eve of remembered history, enormous prestige attached to the man who could defend his community against the incursions of predatory animals." (77)

There have also been great advances in thought along the way as Man questioned his place in the universe.

Unfortunately Man has turned away from himself and toward technology. Our advances in technology over the past two thousand years have been staggering. They are accelerating at a mind numbing speed. We have not, however, advanced our Being in a like manner. Someone might argue that we live longer due to our medicines and living conditions but even that is debatable. There is ample evidence to suggest we do not. It depends on whose statistical mumbo-jumbo you wish to believe. I just look at all the famous historical figures and the venerable ages they attained to choose my bias. The man of today is not more advanced (physiologically, psychologically, pneumatologically) than our ancestors (i.e. Renaissance men). Once you sit down and read some of the ancient texts of nearly every culture you could make the argument that they were at least more mentally and spiritually gifted. And if you look at the waist size of the average American the physical isn't much of stretch either. I am not suggesting abandoning technology altogether. That would be like throwing the baby out with the bath water, but we do need balance. It is time to recognize the error of our ways and make up for lost time as Peter Lavenda states in *Unholy Alliance*,

> "Darwin saw evolution as a force of nature and, in a sense; it is therefore also a force of history. We may be living in an age where the very essence of a human being is undergoing a subtle - perhaps psychic - change. It is said that humans are the only creatures who are conscious of their own inevitable death; that what differentiates us from the rest of the animal kingdom is the certain knowledge that we will one day die. Perhaps now, after Darwin we have also become the only creatures who know that they are a *process*, creatures constantly in the state of becoming." (330)

That is exactly what this book is about, and why we need the Dark Arts of Immortality to take Man to the apex of personal development.

Aim of Man

It appears Aristotle was right that the highest aim for Man is his own self-realization. What could possibly be more valuable? Yes I know, that sounds selfish. To a degree maybe it is, but from another perspective it makes perfect sense. Somehow over the years we equated selfish with evil. Nothing could be farther from the truth. Without a high regard for one's self, nothing is possible. Belief in one's self is of paramount necessity and directly proportional in most cases to the level of success at overcoming challenges. Nietzsche has it right when he says,

> "All the beauty and sublimity we have bestowed upon real and imaginary things I will reclaim as the property and product of man: as his fairest apology. Man as poet, as thinker, as God, as love, as power: with what regal liberality he has lavished gifts upon things so as to impoverish himself and make himself feel wretched!" (85)

Man has given up himself in the name of civilization, even though there is nothing civil about it. Most of the greatest accomplishments in human history started out as acts of selfishness (i.e. the numerous "discoveries" of the Americas). Meanwhile, some of the greatest atrocities have been committed in the name of the selfless (i.e. the Crusades). Don't confuse the idea of selfishness with detriment to society either. If all everyone did, was what appeared to benefit only the collective, the individual Man would fade into obscurity. And so would most great accomplishments. It is possible, in fact probable, that all men will benefit from the discoveries of the selfish man. Keep in mind, the line between good and evil and right and wrong is not as clear as you have been led to believe.

If we imagine for a minute a higher man, what would his powers be? What abilities would he have that we do not have now? We could end up with some very different ideas here, depending on who answers the questions. It could range from as little as adding an inch to height to as much as omnipotence. What is really important here is that Man should want to improve and should act to do so. He should acquire abilities that facilitate this first and foremost beyond nearly all other possible activities. Powers that will enable him to ask better questions, come up with better answers, and enact better solutions. The Dark Arts are the tools needed to develop those powers. Improvement has been programmed into our nature, but often the energy generated has been misdirected. Self-realization is the aim of Man. It always has been and always will be. Until Man embraces this philosophy he will be lost in the light of the selfless. It is time to choose. Ouspensky warns in *The Psychology of Man's Possible Evolution*,

> "Our fundamental idea shall be that man as we know him *is not a completed being*; that nature develops him only up to a certain point and then leaves him, to develop further, *by his own* efforts and devices, or to live and die such as he was born, or to degenerate and lose capacity for development." (pg8)

It is obvious you are on the path to improvement. Know this: all men will benefit from your example.

Ouspensky continues in *Tertium Organum*,

> "The shadows of a sailor, a hangman and a saint may be completely identical - it is impossible to distinguish them by their shadows... These men seem to us alike and equal cause, in general; we see *only the shadows* of real facts. In reality, the 'souls' of these men are totally different, and different not in quality, not in magnitude, not in their 'age' as people prefer to put in now, but different *in their very nature, their origin and the purpose of their existence...*" (129)

It is this power to determine our development that must be utilized to bring us to a unique existence. The proof of your uniqueness lies in your life here. Your experiences, your ideas, your desires... There will certainly be similarities, things several individuals share, but we should not all be striving for identical identity of spirit any more that we do for personality.

Genes, Memes, Esses

Genes are the building blocks of Homo sapiens. The blueprint for construction is called DNA. Think of DNA as an encyclopedia set describing how to build a human, it is divided into 46 volumes (23 pairs) called chromosomes. Those volumes contain a total of about 40,000 sentences of instruction. Those sentences are genes and they build proteins. In the cell those sentences replicate themselves to create more cells. There are several different methods of replication in nature. They are primarily attraction, imitation, and contagion. Genes replicate by splitting up and attracting opposite halves back to make two complete units. A gene basically uses this replicating method to transmit its information into more cells and these groups form organisms, kind of a collective. This idea leads us to the discussion of memes as imitators and esses as contagion (replicators), the first being related to ideas and the latter to emotions.

One of the ways man attempts to understand himself is by studying the institutions of men. The idea is that those groups of organized humans will shed light on the nature of the individual man. One of the more interesting concepts to come out of this study of late is the idea of self-replicating systems and superorganisms, both related to the appearance of self-interest (consciousness) in a non-sentient entity. These are strong indicators of the ideas related to human drives and spirit. The three concepts we will discuss are genes, memes, and esses. Howard Bloom explains it this way,

> "Genes sit at the center of each cellular blob, dictating the construction of a multibillion-celled body like yours and mine. As genes are to the organism, so memes are to the superorganism, pulling together millions of individuals into a collective creature of awesome size. Memes stretch their tendrils through the fabric of each human brain, driving us to coagulate in the cooperative masses of family, tribe, and nation. And memes - working together in theories, worldviews, or cultures - can make a superorganism very hungry." (pg98).

Memes in this context are related to the subjective world. They are the ideas that stick in someone's mind, linking like-minded individuals together creating, for example, a nation (superorganism). The meme in this case could be communism. The original concept by Richard Dawkins who coined the word 'meme' was to represent cultural practices and traditions. It seemed to him they self-replicated like genes combining people like the cells of a body to create nations (superorganism). Howard Bloom separates the term memes from its cultural connections and shows that the idea (i.e. communism) can take root in any group through imitation. He points out that the idea (meme) does not even have to be right, only conducive to bringing people together by replicating and killing off or assimilating counter ideas (i.e. democracy) in a process of seeking dominance.

I created the term esse to satisfy a condition I felt was not ideological but related more to emotion. It is a contagion that disregards reason. You ever notice how someone's mood can affect yours. Laughter makes people laugh and crying makes people sad, etc. Esses vie for their own form of control and replication. They ignore genes and memes and create an invisible 'spirit' of their own. War is a good example of enactment of an esse. War transcends religion but it further transcends culture, genetics and just about everything else. It is entirely common for enemy soldiers to have a certain respect and even camaraderie towards one another, which is inexplicable from a rational standpoint considering the situation. War is its own master. Memes do not use it; it uses them (and us). It is no meme because no one in their right mind would choose to go to war, it is an esse, an inexplicable contagious desire that overcomes all reason. It is not an idea in the subjective realm like a meme and it does not bring people together under that guise (although obviously people joined together will use war). Ehrenreich comes closer with:

> "However and wherever war begins, it persists, it spreads, it propagates itself through time and across space with the terrifying tenacity of a beast attached to the neck of living prey. This is not an idly chosen figure of speech. War spreads and perpetuates itself

through a dynamic that often seems independent of human will. It has, as we like to say of things we don't fully understand, 'a life of its own.'" (132)

There are certainly other esses and their roots lie in the Noujective world. One that comes to mind is sex. It has drawn together two of the most different groups on the planet, men and women. Esses are related to emotions. They certainly replicate themselves similarly to genes and memes. They utilize some of the same processes of imitation, attraction, and contagion. They are definitely at the root of war, sex, and magic.

You should consider this chapter a warning. It is time to evaluate what memes and esses are controlling you. They are seeking expression of uniqueness. They want to survive long enough to spread. Bloom explains this best in *The Lucifer Principle*,

> "Behind the writhing of evil is a competition between organizational devices, each trying to harness the universe to its own peculiar pattern, each attempting to hoist the cosmos one step higher on a ladder of increasing complexity. First, there is the molecular replicator, the gene; then, there is its successor the meme; and working hand in hand with each is the social beast." (pg325)

What they are doing unconsciously, we should be doing consciously.

If you need an example just take a look at the $160 sneaker (Nike, Adidas). Why in the world would parents buy tennis shoes that cost that much for kids? Advertisers and filmmakers are masters of memes and esses. Once you have a handle on how you are being manipulated by your beliefs, it will be time to change them. We are going to harness their power for our own ends. Belief is the most powerful tool you have in your arsenal and it determines the effectiveness of all work.

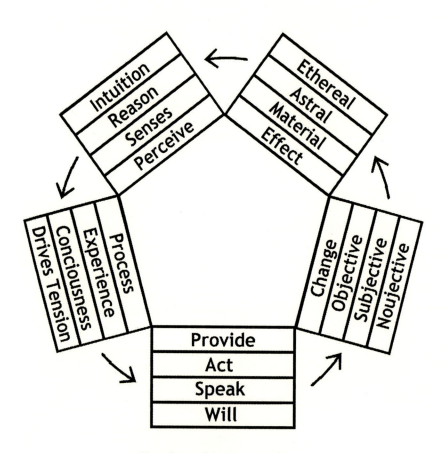

Cycle of Interaction

III. Cycle of Interaction

*The truly free man chooses his own goals and seeks his own ends,
purely for the joy of the choice and the seeking.*
                                              -MATTHEW STOVER

There are three ways in which you can affect the Universe. You are constantly faced with decisions to make based on the situation in which you find yourself. Some are of your own making from earlier choices, some not. Some are seemingly random events that come out of nowhere, and always when you least expect it. Our perception of the Universe comes from our five senses, reasoned thought processes, and intuition. We process this information based on past experiences, our level of consciousness, and tension within our drives. The changes caused within our three worlds impacts our choice of reaction. We are always involved in a certain context. As they say 'no man is an island'. Our interaction with the world around us is in constant flux. Never quite settling down, never completely predictable, and never, never, exactly what we want. That is because every action or non-action alters world possibilities. Every choice reveals new opportunities to be seized or not as the actor sees fit. Recognizing and capitalizing on these opportunities requires a super-human effort and focus.

Regardless of the cause for the predicament you find yourself in you really only have three ways to change it. You can act in such a way as to cause change, you can speak in such a way as to cause change, and you can will in such a way as to cause change. Any combination of the three will work but clearly the most effective method is to utilize all of them. The idea of action should be relatively easy to understand. Action is when you physically cause something to occur in an attempt to make the outcome fit with your intent. When I refer to speaking it includes all forms of communication (written, body language). Basically it is an attempt to pass on information to another mind in order to get a reaction or response. There is no denying the power of verbalizing a desire of course but many other methods are in use all around you all the time communicating to your mind whether you like it or not.

Using will to create an effect is a little more complicated to explain. Suffice it to say that your attitude about a given situation will alter the outcome for better or worse. Sometimes the influence it has is great and sometimes nearly insignificant but it has its effect none-the-less. Ask any military commander about the power of morale and he will be able to articulate will very clearly. I am sure you have had an experience that can reflect this point. Some incident where it took you an incredible amount of willpower to be successful and without it would have meant failure. Or a failure you had simply because someone else wanted it more than you did at the time. Just like the light spectrum the invisible world is much larger than the world we see.

It is this world of invisible forces we are influencing with our force of being. We are going to attempt to harness such "stuff" for our own empowerment. There is a basic essence to the Universe we can detect on a personal level, but science is still trying to figure it out. They are getting closer as they investigate evidence that observation can alter results of tests, but we can never have a complete scientific picture of the world. Mainly because science only deals with parts that it can measure. It leaves out more than in includes.

Action emanates from and is most powerful in man's Objective world, speech in the Subjective and will in the Noujective but each reverberates throughout the others. Remember you are a part of the Universe (All-That-Is/Is-Not) so any change within yourself counts as affecting It. If improvement is made at any point in the cycle of interaction (perception to effect), then a corresponding improvement will be made in the results. The first and most powerful improvement that anyone can make is to combine action, speech, and will toward any end they have in mind. Of course the higher man will work to improve all areas of perception, processing, etc.

Cause and Effect

To our normal experience, the every day world seems like a series of chaotic and totally unrelated events. We are constantly bombarded by ripples in the pond of the Material dimension from the pebbles other people have carelessly tossed into it. We sometimes think we recognize secret forces controlling these events. We have phrases to describe this such as "luck" or principles like "Murphy's Law," but the truth is much more sinister: the Universe does not care about you. Learn to live with it.

It is a world of infinite causes and effects. The chain of results from a single action is immeasurable. We drop a piece of paper on the way out of the office. Stopping to pick it up causes the person behind us to delay leaving the building by a couple seconds. They get in their car and start driving home. They arrive at an intersection just when a pedestrian steps out. The driver swerves to avoid him and the car hits a light pole causing a power outage and signal problems. Now dozens of people's routines are disrupted and all their actions take place at times different from what would have happened originally. Ripples go out in a thousand different directions. There is no way to measure the impact that piece of paper had on the world. In addition to the obvious effects, there are a multitude of invisible forces at work as well. Some we are familiar with like gravity, magnetism, and chemical reactions we don't really think about on a conscious level. For all the ones we understand and recognize there are still many that remain hidden from our sophisticated scientific observations. All of these causes (forces) create effects that each person encounters every second of every day of every year. Even thoughts and emotions are under the influence of cause and effect. That form of causality is just much more obscure.

Very few of us pay close attention to our daily lives. We drift through them half-sleeping. Gaining some direction and control over our lives requires work. Firm direction and control is exactly what we desire. We want the power to alter effects in a manner that more consistently conforms to our intent and more frequently results in positive outcomes for ourselves an others, more win-win. This power is not going to come easily, but the rewards will be remarkable. This capability not only creates a more enjoyable life, but it also opens up more freedom for the individual. Peter J. Carroll points out,

> "Liberating behavior is that which increases one's possibilities for future action. Limiting behavior is that which tends to narrow one's options. The secret of freedom is not to be drawn into situations where one's number of alternatives becomes limited or even unitary." (45)

He is right. But the only way 'not to be drawn into' bad situations is to better control the outcomes of your decisions. Liberating behavior does lead to freedom by opening up possibilities. But it also leads to one other thing, power. True power is not control over someone else, but the control you have over how his or her causes affect you. The more we liberate ourselves from the effects of other people and the uncaring Universe the closer we move toward divinity (DAIS).

Act

The first way we affect the Universe is through action. The material dimension surrounds us. The objects we encounter in our immediate vicinity and which we perceive and interact with is our Objective world. Each person has an Objective world that is unique to him or her in totality but may overlap and interact with other people's Objective world. By acting on objects in our surroundings we put effects into play, which in turn cause other effects. Gunter Figal defines this as a type of freedom: "We are free because all of our actions necessarily belong to a world that freely releases action and that cannot be exhausted by any single action. We are free in that we open ourselves in the world to the possibilities that are accessible to us." (18).

Although it often appears things are out of our control, action actually gives us the best chance of having events match our intent. We continually have direct impact on the Universe through our actions or lack thereof. Our actions not only impact the Material dimension but also the Objective worlds of others. If someone perceives our action or the results of our action, it sends a message to their Subjective and Noujective worlds as well. Obviously any action is also perceived by us as feedback and so affects our Subjective and Noujective worlds (an action that succeeds strengthens it). When we say act, we are talking about everything from playing football to mixing ingredients for a cake. This is the most underutilized ability Man has. He wastes a lot of potential by failing to act.

Speak

When I talk about speaking I am really referring to all forms of communication from speech, to the written word, symbols, and even body language. Thought is the primary function of the Subjective world. Speech is the best way of affecting the subjective world of others because it creates changes in thoughts and may motivate action or a change in behavior. Many ancient peoples from European magicians to Native Americans believed sound itself has a direct impact on the Material dimension. They thought that by speaking certain words of power or chanting runes or songs in just the right manner would change lead into gold or create storm clouds over a desert wasteland. You laugh. But are you completely positive that they had no effect? Can you prove it? Some scientists suggest the Universe is made of vibrating string particles. Who knows what might be accomplished with the proper voice modulation and air vibratory rates. If there is a slim possibility it had some effect then why not improve your odds?

Certainly the vibration of air and whatever invisible mental pulses occur have their effect on the Universe. Whether we comprehend them currently or not is immaterial to the matter at hand. Others admit that speaking something out loud increases the chances of it occurring tenfold. What all of this hits on is a simple fact that communicating your desires improves the probability of success.

Of greater import for our work here we go to Anton Szandor LaVey in *The Satanic Bible* when he says, "Despite all non-verbalists' protests to the contrary, soaring heights of emotional ecstasy or raging pangs of anguish can be attained through verbal communication." (143). He must have understood people well, considering the impact talking dirty has on us sexually. We also see success within the realm of self-improvement. Self talk and internal communication can completely change the belief in a manner impossible in any other way. Not to mention the impact body language has not only on other observers but on your own mood as well. Smiling can change your emotion even if you are not happy. All manner of communication is how the subjective world conveys information between beings and to the Universe.

The changes wrought in the Astral and Ethereal dimensions go without saying, although identification may be much more difficult because, as P. D. Ouspensky explains in *Tertium Organum*:

> "The fact of the matter is that *thought* and *energy* [emotion] are different in their essence and cannot be *one and the same thing* because they are different aspects of the same thing. If we were to open the skull of a living man and see all the vibrations in the cells of the gray matter of the brain and all the quiverings of the white matter, it would still be only motion, i.e. manifestations of energy, and thought would remain somewhere beyond the field of investigation, receding from it at every approach, like a shadow." (122)

Will

The word will has several uses in our language. Many meanings frequently get overlooked and confused especially when crossing fields of study (i.e. philosophy to psychology). As it was defined in the first chapter (the power of choosing: the faculty or endowment of the spirit by which it is capable of choosing) it is clear that will is tied to the spirit, which in turn is connected to the noujective part of man and his drives and emotions. You are probably used to associating it with words like tenacity, endurance, discipline, etc. These words are certainly fitting for the symptomatic manifestations of will, but they are not will itself. It usually manifests in association with intense emotions, and this is when its energy is most apparent.

Will is an intangible force and as such we rarely harness it intentionally. It can be associated with words like pneuma (spirit), anima (soul), and certainly with noumenal (conceive) and numinous (holy). We can recognize it in our daily life through attraction, personal chemistry or magnetism, as well as in those people that have charisma. Some people exhibit a level of confidence that causes things to simply fall into place and people around them to be attracted for no obvious reason. In ancient times the Germanic people called this hamingja; meaning "luck". Because of this force, events seemed to go their way and people followed them. Great leaders were followed as much for their skills as they were for the belief they were lucky. Strong belief shows in the will. It is connected to the spirit, and most people have experienced it but may not be sure how to define what they know. I am sure if you think a little while you can come up with an event in your life when you experienced this power, such as a time when you were very angry, or desperate. Obvious uses of will 'power' might be clear now. The will reinforces action and it strengthens speech and is a direct expression of the Noujective world of Man. There is also a hidden aspect of will in the Dark Arts of Immortality that leads directly to ascension.

Dimension Crossover

I have already alluded to the way the Universe is divided into three dimensions (Material, Astral, and Ethereal). It is apparent now that man bridges all three. Everything man does impacts his three worlds (Objective, Subjective, and Noujective). These in turn each impact the dimension where they reside (Material, Astral, and Ethereal respectively). If man bridges the dimensions, then from what we know of energy is it possible to understand other objects from the Material dimension having connections to the Astral and Ethereal as well. In fact they most assuredly do, even if it is only through man. Form, idea, and essence are the counterparts (to the worlds of man) for non-sentient objects and abstract concepts.

We can agree that action, speech, and willing are the three ways we affect the Universe. We can certainly see how we can speak to our own Subjective world to affect change. We can probably agree that speaking can affect other Subjective worlds. Can we also agree that actions affect our Subjective world and other Subjective worlds? Feedback from actions can reinforce or challenge our thinking, so our conclusion would have to be yes. Actions also affect the Subjective worlds of those who are directly affected by them as well as individuals effected by ripples in the future that don't know what caused them.

So actions affect Objective and Subjective worlds. Speech affects Subjective worlds and feedback from speech affects actions, hence objective impact. So likewise, even without the direct effect of vibrations from vocalization manifesting change in the Objective world, we can still conclude that it does affect it.

It is not much of a stretch to say that actions affect the Noujective world as well (although difficult to prove since it is hidden from us) through drive tension and emotions. In fact, it is probably closer to a rational conclusion than a stretch. It is much easier though to understand how speech impacts the Noujective. Self-talk is used to empower the self in many circumstances especially overcoming challenges. To help understand how the subjective impacts the Noujective lets look at a situation. Have you ever given words of praise to someone for a job well done? Your words, smile, and eye contact all communicate something positive and the person lit up. That spark was the Noujective. Have you ever had someone try to intimidate you? They use mean expressions and body language, harsh words, etc. If they were successful they sapped your will. If conflict had ensued you would have been less likely to defeat the person due to this effect. However if it didn't bother you they probably strengthened your resolve and would have been more likely to get their block knocked off. Either way, it impacted your Noujective world.

From this discussion we can say that action, speech, and will affect all three worlds of Man and all three dimensions of the Universe. A person is who truly Being combines action, speech, and will in all they do. They engage all three worlds (Objective, Subjective, Noujective) in their everyday existence in order to give their intent full power. This is one of the problems alluded to in an earlier discussion. We think we have abilities we don't. We believe we have knowledge of something we don't. We intend to control things we can't. Man has a mistaken belief about a great many of his powers and faculties. It isn't that we cannot acquire these abilities, that knowledge, and total control, it is simply that we have not done so. We don't work on gaining those characteristics because we assume we already have them. Not to mention the difficulty involved in achieving powers we know we don't have currently. That is another matter entirely but at least we know we need to work on those vs. the not knowing of something we think we have.

Of course, most people use only a fraction of their potential in any give situation, but delude themselves into believing they are giving one hundred percent. Simply by engaging the practice of using all three techniques (act, speak, will) to cause a desired effect in the Universe will grant us an ability we 'think' we already possess. A person just using one world is not fully awake or empowered and tends to rely on a singular (or no) approach to any situation. When encountering another individual, a human Being will attempt to engage all of that person's worlds in order to have the greatest influence. If the dimensions overlay each other and influence each other it would make sense to cause as much conformity between the microcosm and the macrocosm as possible to ensure the greatest possibility of success.

Libido, Mortido, Physis

Psychologists, sociologists, and theologians have argued over the prime movers of human beings since our earliest development. They termed them drives since they seem to propel us in a certain direction. The three drives are Libido, Mortido, and Physis (the sex, death, and growth drive). They equate to a tension that builds up in the organism until it is expressed (released through some doing). They create a physiological, psychological, as well as pneumatalogical tension that must be released through some activity related to it. Over the years their definitions have remained somewhat consistent but different psychologists tried to classify two or more of them together. Some combine physis with libido, libido and mortido by others, and of course Freud combined everything under libido. For him sex was all-powerful. The three distinct divisions question will clear up itself as we investigate the nature of each drive but there is another problem. There is serious doubt as to whether these are actually rooted in the psyche, as it is now defined. The original word psyche meant something closer to spirit and it is most likely the drives are rooted in the Noujective and cause effects in physiology, psychology, and pneumatology. The pneumatological origins are especially important because they are the most difficult to understand. Yet they are possibly the most valuable to our current work.

Libido is a tension that equates to sex and has often been termed the sex drive. Of the three, it is the easiest to understand although arguably the hardest to control. Which is probably why Freud put everything under its dominion. It is connected to the experience of pleasure and its primary satisfaction is achieved through orgasm. Some believe its purpose is procreation and propagation of the species. Dawkins would argue that genes are using us for their own ends. Either way, it tends to pull us together and is accordingly considered creative and cooperative in nature. It covers our desire to obtain pleasure and to replicate our genetic structure. For our purposes we will focus on the pleasure aspect of libido and often refer to it as the sex drive.

Mortido is a little more complicated but simply put Mortido is a tension that equates to killing. Its primary satisfaction is achieved through violence. It is related to separation and destruction. Its purpose is self-preservation (both defensive and predatory). The drive for violence stems from our primal biological need to kill for food. As Howard Bloom points out,

> "Killing is an invention not of man but of nature. ...Nature has made that form of tragedy a basic law of her universe. She presents her children with a choice between death and death. She offers a carnivore the options of dying by starvation or killing for a meal." (25)

In order to survive we must kill plants and animals to eat. We must have a powerful drive to force us to confront dangerous animals without natural weapons of our own and to overcome the guilt associated with predation. Anthropologists may argue over whether other animals ever preyed upon man, but that would be another reason for a powerful drive. Evidence points to the distinct possibility of predation by the big cats on early man. In fact they are still the number one animal kingdom killers of humans today. This could explain the reverence afforded them in the worship of Freya by the Germanic people. Another explanation for this drive is the competition for food. Though, rarely in the animal kingdom does a duel for dominion (of a pack, territory, harem, etc.) end in death for the defeated, death occurs because only the winners eat. A simple act of violence may squelch the tension even if it is competitive and not mortal in nature. The greatest acts of violence are those of self-preservation, so we will speak of mortido (the death drive) in those terms. Man was not born with great natural weapons such as large teeth, claws, or horns, but he has an advantage in biology when it comes to the mind and tool use (escalation of power). If he chooses to control his fear he can increase his physical abilities through rage and his capability through weapons. Regardless, Man certainly preys on his own kind as well as other animals. It is possible the death drive (predation) took a turn for the worse when we began agriculture and especially the domestication of animals. We no longer needed to hunt for food as much and that drive just found another source of expression (war). During the periods of prehistory when well-equipped predators preyed upon us this drive was our protection. As carnivores we also needed the instinct to kill for food and this drive helped us become predators. When man became agrarian, he directed all attention to war and now battle is where mortido gets its greatest satisfaction so we often call it the death drive.

Physis is a tension that equates to personal improvement. It is most clearly felt in the anxiety of boredom. Of the three drives, it is the most difficult to understand and the fact that many psychologists tried to lump it in to either Mortido or Libido did not help. It is related to ambition, freedom, and learning (search for the unknown). Its original conception included the life principle of healing but moved more toward the idea of individual evolution. It is the desire for more, for strife as we discussed earlier, for that challenge which allows us to become better. It is the antithesis of the status quo. In reference to this concept Figal says,

> "*Will to power* is the name for the dynamic of life, posited as a principle, which holds only for what serves to augment it. The will to power is a will, which does not fulfill itself in any goal, but only in itself, that is to say, in the possibility of exceeding its current state." (162)

Its purpose is realized in the quest for self-transformation. Its greatest satisfaction is achieved through victory and domination primarily although, not exclusively, of one's self. Aristotle's position was that our quest is endless. We do one thing to get something else only to continue to do and get. He believed the highest aim for man was to realize his full potential. To become all that he could become. He equated this with good but we will address our definition of good and evil later. Just keep in mind that the entire Universe mimics this same process of acquiring more. To ensure this aim has the potential for actualization homo sapiens, humans have a built in mechanism for attainment. Because of its relationship to personal development it is often called the Growth drive.

If any drive goes unexpressed it builds up a form of pressure within the individual. This pressure seeks relief through enactment of the things that fulfill its satisfaction. The length of time for that pressure to build up to an uncomfortable level is different for each person. Enactment that satisfies one drive can siphon off some of that collective tension but not enough to keep it at a low level. Think of it like a swimming pool with three hoses and three drains. The three hoses run all the time filling the pool. One drain may be able to keep the water from overflowing for a while, but it really takes all three to keep the proper level. This is one reason there is so much turmoil within people. They do not keep a balance in the satisfaction of their drives because they attempt to suppress them or to satisfy one by expressing another. Again, this may work for the short term but not for long. Another problem arises when proper activity isn't used to relieve the tension because we misunderstand the needs of the drive. For example everyone is familiar with lack of sexual release seeking expression in anger or people becoming workaholics because they have no releases for libido and mortido. There is also a difficulty in processing information and experience when the drive tensions are imbalanced. People cannot think clearly when this physiological, psychological, and pneumatological pressure is overwhelming. It is imperative to get this under control in order to elevate Being. There is so much wasted potential within this facet of human existence. It is time to harness this power toward our own ends by harmonizing the drives, our nature, and our aims.

So where can we look to help us in our search for understanding the use of our drives? Jacobi explains Jung's position this way in *The Psychology of C. G. Jung*:

> "Thus for Jung the archetypes [myths, folk tales] taken as a whole represent the sum of the latent potentialities of the human psyche - a vast store of ancestral knowledge about the profound relations between God[s], man, and cosmos. To open up this store in one's own psyche, to awaken it to new life and integrate it with consciousness, means nothing less that to save the individual from his isolation and gather him into the eternal cosmic process. Thus the conceptions of which we have been speaking become more than a science and more that a psychology. They become a way of life. The archetype as the primal source of all human experience lies in the unconscious [subconscious], whence it reaches into our lives. Thus it becomes imperative to resolve its projections, to raise its contents to consciousness." (48)

We can see the drives at work in ancient texts. These stories hold a key to understanding our selves and the use of our drives. It is necessary 'to raise its contents to consciousness' in fact to supra-consciousness. This is deep-seated primal knowledge and we will go into it in more depth in another chapter. We can also refer back to our discussion of human social interaction in the section on genes, memes, and esses. Remember these groups create superorganisms that mimic the nature of the individual. There is ample evidence of the drives exhibited within nearly all human institutions. But as with genes, memes, and esses we need to make sure we are controlling and utilizing them toward our interests instead of the other way around.

Power of Choice

> "Life is a game. A game consists of *freedom, barriers,* and *purposes.* This is a scientific fact, not merely an observation. ...the ability to play a game consists of tolerance for freedom and barriers and an insight into purposes, with the power of choice over participation." (62)

L. Ron Hubbard is not the first person to identify life as a game. In fact it has often been called the 'master game'. He does however identify the prime choice of humanity. To play or not to play, that is the question.

One of the greatest powers we have as humans is the ability to choose. Next to belief, this is probably the most important power we have. Unlike the laws of nature and the patterned behavior of animals when it comes to causal relationships we are the only beings we know of that have the option of redirecting its path and changing the Universe consciously. I realize that some would argue that our decision making process is fundamentally a cause and effect relationship as well but it does not operate under exactly the same laws and principles. Certainly things have happened in our past experiences or in our education that determines the choices we will make, thus somewhat causal. So, it may be true to an extent, but the real importance here is that the more conscious we are of ourselves and our capabilities, the more likely we are to alter events to better suit our needs and less likely to decide out of habit.

Don Webb suggests the common condition of human beings in *Uncle Setnakt's Essential Guide to the Left Hand Path*, "They have been taught - or rather acquired - a series of randomly assorted thoughts, notions, and behaviors most of which either actively hinder them, or at best lull them into a sleeplike state." (3). Due to this 'sleeplike' condition, a lot of possibilities never come to fruition. Whether we use this power of choice or not is up to us. We can try new things and create new opportunities. We can overcome programming and habits by choice, or we can allow them free reign. Keep in mind that not choosing is still choosing; namely choosing not to choose. Choosing not-to-choose is a common selection for most people because it is easier to just let things happen, especially if conditions are tolerable. Of course when someone consciously makes choices between various possibilities it is incumbent upon them to take responsibility for the outcomes and to justify their choice in light of them. This justification is either the process of selecting the course of action one wishes to take based on a predicted result, or it is the explanation after the fact of why it was selected based on consequences. Both of these require accountability, which is a dirty word in the average person's vocabulary. Being 'asleep' makes this process easier to deal with because no effort is required, just acceptance of the outcomes (as long as they are tolerable) which is often easier than the effort required to choose consciously. The flaw of course in this type of undirected choosing is that life becomes dull. We become frustrated because the very reasons we don't choose become the very mechanisms by which life eventually becomes more difficult to bear.

Ask any woman why she prefers dating a bad boy versus a nice guy. Her answer will be because nice guys are boring. It is the tension created by ups and downs in a relationship that make it exciting. Stagnation is a passion killer.

Emotional connections need danger, taboo, and roughness mixed in with the normal intimate commitments or it will lack texture and delight. Women will relish the bad times because they make the good moments delicious.

The Germanic concepts of wyrd and orlog are tied up with the concept of fate. Fate is defined as the principle or determining cause or will by which things in general are believed to come to be as they are or events to happen as they do. Orlog is the pattern that has been laid down already in the past and wyrd is the direction it is currently going. Contrary to common understanding, the Germanic peoples did not believe in predestination. They did not see things as having to happen a predetermined way, only likely to happen a certain way because of the paradigm in place. It is tied to this habit of behavior just mentioned. The future is a direct result of a pattern that emerges out of history and likely to repeat unless broken by some choice. So a man could change his destiny but he is unlikely to do so because he will typically make the same decisions to the same stimulus.

Everyone has the only power they need to accomplish anything in life (or death). That power is the power of choice. The right choices in life will bring you to any destiny you desire. There is some combination of choices that can make it happen. You do not need willpower, discipline, luck, etc. All you need to do is choose. Hubbard further suggests: "Despite the amount of suffering, pain, misery, sorrow and travail which can exist in life, the reason for existence is the same reason as one has to play a game - interest, contest, activity and possession." (61). If you wish to make life interesting, to win the contest, to enjoy the activity, and to obtain all that you want... choose.

Cycle of Interaction

The first step in utilizing the power of choice is to identify the Cycle of Interaction between your inner and outer worlds. This is basically the process of obtaining information or knowledge, processing it into a decision, and then providing some doing based on that choice. The doing will cause an effect on the Material, Astral, and Ethereal dimensions of the Universe. The feedback we receive will cause a change in our Objective, Subjective and Noujective worlds. We have already discussed the three ways we affect the Universe, so lets take a look at our thinking and being in relation to doing and the effects wrought on the Self.

The first area we need to come to grips with is how we perceive the Universe. It will effect how we proceed. Peter J. Carroll in *Liber Null & Psychonaut* sites the importance of perception:

> "...I saw that in the innermost core of my being there was only the power of will and the power of perception. Everything else was added on and could be stripped away. I began to see that under the apparent order of matter there was a spontaneous, creative, chaotic, magical force at work. These insights at first appalled me and it was some years before I accepted and confirmed them." (202)

The knowledge we gain from perception and the accuracy of those perceptions will be the first and crucial step in the cycle.

The three methods of perceiving the world are the senses, reason, and intuition. Everyone is familiar with the five senses: visual (sight), auditory (sound), gustatory (taste), kinesthetic (feel), and olfactory (smell). Reason refers to the thinking process itself, and it is an activity of perception that goes on exclusively within the mind. It is the process of logic and deduction. Intuition is the third perceptive faculty. Although intuition is separate from logic, it is not to be considered a better nor worse method of perceiving, only different in kind. It is also not faith (I will not insult your intelligence by suggesting you accept something without evidence and consider it a higher form of thinking). It is more accurate to say true (or full) perception can only be achieved with the inclusion of intuition. Intuition is a form of direct knowledge. This faculty is hidden from us in our Noujective world, but just because we don't fully understand its mechanisms doesn't mean we should discount its usefulness. Body and mind processes go on without our awareness all the time, so it should be no surprise if spirit does the same. Just as the five senses can be fooled, and reason can be flawed, so too can intuition be inaccurate; but if all three come to bear on our total perception of the Universe, we will be armed with our most powerful decision making ammunition.

The way in which we process the information gained through perception involves three primary factors: experience, consciousness, and drives tension. Experience includes past involvement with the perceptions received and conditioning as a result as well as the current situation in which one finds them self. Everyone is familiar with experience and it cannot be overestimated. There is almost nothing that can replace it. Consciousness refers to the level of awareness we have at the time of the perception. The three levels of consciousness (subconscious, conscious, supra-conscious) will be addressed later but suffice it to say that some perceptions go on below our normal level of awareness but can still influence our actions and some forms of consciousness are above this same level of mundane awareness. The other factor to be understood is the amount of tension (and in what proportion) has built up from our libido, mortido, and physis (the sex, death, and growth drives discussed earlier). As soon as we use act, speak, and will to produce a change in the self and an effect on the Universe the cycle starts all over again with the feedback.

Perceive	Process	Provide	-	Change	Effect
Senses	Experience	Act	-	Objective	Material
Reason	Consciousness	Speak	-	Subjective	Astral
Intuition	Drives Tension	Will	-	Noujective	Ethereal

If we make an improvement in any part of the cycle we will in turn have an exponential improvement in the results. We can work on paying more attention to our senses, practice our reasoning capability, and recognize our intuitive capacity. We can experience more activities in life, focus our awareness as we engage in them, and recognize and alleviate drive tensions as needed to maintain appropriate balance. The importance of each drive (and each aspect of the cycle for that matter) will vary from individual to individual. Last, but not least, we can use act, speak, and will in conjunction with each other to enhance our doing as discussed earlier. All of these changes increase the power of choice. You are unique and the proportions required to you supply the most benefit will vary from someone else's needs. In order to discover the right harmony requires experimentation and effort. Your ability to perceive, process, and provide is directly proportional to the type of life you will lead and the enjoyment you will get out of living it.

Much of the above cycle happens in the subconscious mind, which has been programmed by the conscious mind and experience. The more of its processes we can perform with full consciousness (or in supra-consciousness), the better. If we can learn to utilize the supra-conscious mind and fully exploit this cycle we will be well on our way to opening the doors to a whole new set of immortal possibilities.

Subconscious, Conscious, Supra-conscious

People go through life asleep. Most individuals don't want to be woke up and will resent you pointing out the fact they are asleep. For those people it would be too difficult and too much work to live in an awakened state. They are so beat down from repeated failures that they no longer have the will necessary to Be. When examining super-organisms Bloom tells why this happens: "Defeat makes super-organisms sleepy. So does poverty. But a military win or a shower of new wealth rouses social energies, inspiring the pecking order instincts to lift their contentious heads. And when a society is aroused, watch out." (263). What he is saying is that failure perpetuates itself, while victory and success do the same thing. Think about it. When you have been aroused to anger by one person and you express that anger through violence. Aren't you more likely to confront other things in your life the same way at that time? When you are lazy and lethargic are you not more likely to engage activities with the same lack. Nations and societies are the same. Once they have a taste for an exciting endeavor they tend to keep that excitement going. When they are beat down they tend to stay that way for a long time.

Another concept that goes along with this is the Hawk and Dove principle. It talks about characteristics of animal behavior. Within any species there are 'hawks' and 'doves', meaning aggressive members and passive members. Hawks are more likely to fight frequently and doves are more likely to submit. Two doves will not usually fight. A hawk confronting a hawk will most often result in conflict. If a hawk confronts a dove the dove will relinquish the territory, food, whatever. If conflict does ensue the victor is more likely to fight again and the loser is less likely (even with regard to two hawks). When you add witnesses it becomes even more convoluted. In this case even a dove will be more likely to fight. Doves may turn into hawks. It fears the idea of being challenged by every other member that has knowledge it will surrender. So it must fight or end up with nothing. This may be why a person asleep does not want anyone recognizing them as a dove and certainly not pointing out to anyone else. Then they will have to fight or lose everything.

To understand awakening you must first realize you are asleep. You will try to argue against this of course, denial is always the first reaction. Do you consider yourself awake when you drive your car or ride your bike? Have you ever started driving home and all of a sudden arrived there but you don't remember anything about the trip? You would normally consider yourself as being awake, but were you? Take a drive somewhere and notice all the things (ads, building, people, etc.) you normally miss along the way because you are asleep. The normal waking state is not being Awake. It is far removed from truly sleeping but is certainly not Awake. To be Awake means to be fully aware of yourself and your surroundings. It is to be aware of feelings, perceptions, actions, and signs entering your field of view impressing images upon your brain. Awake is the only way to Live. We can equate the following levels of wakefulness with the corresponding levels of consciousness. Sleeping is unconsciousness, daydreaming/auto-matic response is sub-consciousness, waking is consciousness, and Awakened is supra-consciousness.

Consciousness is somewhere outside, yet it is dependent on, the organic order for its manifestation as we understand it, and it is here that we will have to work with it. The brain and the mind are not exactly the same thing. Differences in degree lead to differences in kind. Think of the brain like a radio or transducer: it receives power in one mode and then transfers it in another. The brain does not necessarily create consciousness, but it does facilitate its manifestation and it also provides access to the Subjective world. At the same time it receives from and transmits signals to the Objective and Noujective worlds.

Fred Alan Wolf approaches this concept in *Parallel Universes: The Search for Other Worlds* when he says,

> "The laboratory of parallel universe [dimension] experimentation may not lie in a mechanical time machine a la Jules Verne, but could exist between our ears. If the parallel universes [dimensions] of relativity are the same as those of quantum theory the possibility exists that parallel universes [dimensions] may be extremely close to us, perhaps only atomic dimensions away but perhaps in a higher dimension of space - an extension into what physicists call *superspace*. Modern neuroscience, through the study of altered states of awareness, schizophrenia, and lucid dreaming, could be indicating the closeness of parallel worlds to our own." (23)

That is why when you get brain damage things change. Not because all of consciousness is rooted in the organic gray matter, but because it is that construct that interprets the signal and allows for entry into the Material dimension. This would explain many psychological illnesses such as split personality and autism (receiving other signals from the astral dimension or not getting a full signal). It would also explain why we appear to use only a small percentage of our brain's capacity.

Psychologists have debated the nature of consciousness and have developed theory after theory of its divisions and functions. For our purposes we will only be concerned with the following general divisions; unconscious, sub-conscious, conscious, and supra-conscious. Some psychologists use the word unconscious interchangeably with subconscious. For this work unconscious will only be used to apply to the sleeping state where no thought (only dreaming) occurs and this will be the extent of its coverage.

Subconscious will refer to those brain functions and perceptions that go on below our awareness. For example, there are bodily functions such as digestion, circulation, sensory input (such as pheromones) that register on the brain without awareness. Subliminal messages such as body language or those used in advertising could fall in this category. Typically information is stored and accessed in a subconscious manner. The subconscious decides how to file information away and then decides when and if to retrieve it. The subconscious is very important when it comes to performing physical acts, accessing memory, instinctive reactions, and releasing emotions. The subconscious mind allows a lot to go on without control or cluttering awareness.

The term conscious will refer to the normal waking state where we selectively perceive and interpret sensory input. The conscious mind is used to process and analyze information and to train the body for new tasks. Once learned, a task becomes the domain of the subconscious as well (not always a forgone conclusion). The conscious mind broadens awareness and control.

Supra-consciousness is an advanced state of awareness and thought rarely reached by most people. It is naturally occurring in rare circumstances and then usually in a small band of focus that shifts depending on the situation in which it arises. Examples include life threatening situations, extraordinary sexual experiences, etc. (the Zone, Flow, Rapture). As Pauwels and Bergier suggest in *The Morning of the Magicians:*

> "The passage from sleep to a waking state produces a certain number of changes in the body. For example: the arterial tension is different, and there are variations in the nervous impulses. If, as we think, there is another state, which we may call one of super-wakefulness, or super-consciousness, the passage from our normal waking to this super-state must also be attended by transformations of various kinds." (351)

We will spend most of our time in this work discussing this third state of consciousness. Brought to full potential, it will bring preternatural ability in all areas of bodily function, information processing, and emotional release.

Ouspensky explains it in *The Psychology of Man's Possible Evolution* this way,

> "So, in reference to the *third state of consciousness*, we can say that man has occasional moments of self-consciousness leaving vivid memories of the circumstances accompanying them, but he has no command over them. They come and go by themselves, being controlled by external circumstances and occasional associations or memories of emotions. The question arises: is it possible to acquire command over these fleeting moments of consciousness, to evoke them more often, and to keep them longer, or even make them permanent?

In other words, *is it possible to become conscious?* This is the most important point, and it must be understood at the very beginning of our study that this point even as a theory has been entirely missed by all modern psychological schools *without an exception*. For with right methods and the right efforts man *can acquire control of consciousness,* and can *become conscious of himself,* with all that it implies. And what it implies we in our present state do not even imagine." (21)

The Supra-conscious state is on a different order of awareness. It is more capable of perception, emotion, and information processing than the normal waking state. It can also command great abilities from the body, mind, and spirit. The primary states of Being are fury, ecstasy, and exaltation. Unfortunately, these enhanced states have some drawbacks when activated haphazardly. The supra-conscious portion of the mind can be fractured in a way, or it never completely developed in the first place.

Dudley Young did a lot of research into this and discusses the 'alpha-shaman' split in *Origins of the Sacred*. Alpha-shaman could be broken down into warrior, lover, and magus. This is also reflected in the myths and cultural divisions of the Germanic peoples. The Dark Arts unite (or reunite) the separated components through enacting fury, ecstasy, and exaltation on an individual basis. Once unified (through the surpa-conscious, conscious and sub-conscious), these states of Being will function at optimal levels allowing for achievement of peak performance, optimal experience, and hyper emotion with all the benefits and none of the drawbacks. Awareness will broaden, perceptional acuity and physical attributes will increase, time will alter, etc.

Ideally we want to use our conscious mind to train for something and then, once it becomes part of who we are, it passes into the subconscious. This is a reason for experiencing states of supra-consciousness, because those experiences when built up over a long period will become part of the subconscious. This overall consciousness will allow these powers (or anything for that matter) to become natural making them more likely to occur when desired with little effort.

IV. Left Hand Path

*...humans are but machines,
but in potential may become gods.*
-Don Webb

With regard to immortality we look at existence with one of two views. That Man is a process of refinement for the soul (for those who believe in reincarnation or a pre-existing soul), or a machine for the creation of one. In either case, you can see the importance of your life in the here and now. As for the former, the fact you were drawn to this work indicates this is your last incarnation in that process and you should approach it that way. You should attempt to use this information to complete your cycle of rebirth. If it is the latter then this is the only chance you get to create a Masterpiece. Just as the Universe is made up of the interactions between the three dimensions (Material, Astral, Ethereal), each man is the unity of interaction of his three worlds (Objective, Subjective, Noujective). In order to affect the Universe, man needs only to work in one dimension. In order to change his Being man must make a change to one of his worlds. The most powerful effects and profound changes, though, will be generated when all three worlds (dimensions) are worked in concert, whether to change the Self or affect the Universe.

When you look at each action there is no way to tell whether it will be ultimately good or evil over the long run. A good intention may create evil results, and vice versa an evil intention can turn out good consequences. In all likelihood most causes will have both effects. This dichotomy has led to some of the most pretentious and disastrous practices of mankind. Man has fallen away from trust in his own abilities and common sense due to the apparent unpredictability of results. He has to ask permission from someone else for everything to avoid being labeled by his peers and criticized by supposed professionals. It is time to reclaim personal power and take responsibility for our selves. Black and Dr. Hyatt put it beautifully in *Pacts with the Devil* by saying,

> "To refuse the services of the politician, the priest, or the psychiatrist is an insult - to them. To negotiate for yourself, to be your own priest, your own psychiatrist, your own politician, is sacrilege, insanity or

criminality. What label they apply to you is a function of who has the most power as well as the accident of who apprehends you first..." (13)

One of the worst creations of this line of thinking is a loss of belief in the Self. We no longer teach people to think for themselves. We are fractured Beings. We need a specialist to tell us everything. Because of this lower status, man has lost site of one of the main branches of religion. Most people are not familiar with the terms Right Hand Path and Left Hand Path. They refer to the type of immortal existence one achieves by practicing a particular theology. Nearly, all modern religions teach a philosophy of the Right Hand Path. This means that upon death of the individual they will be absorbed into the Godhead. On-the-other-hand (no pun intended), the teachings of the Left-Hand Path lead to an immortal existence of the individual identity, a sort of divine ascension whereby you become a god (Divinely Ascended Immortal Soul). The Right Hand Path is used to pacify and control people and in the end it leads toward relinquishing of Being. The Left Hand Path is directed toward elevation of Being through becoming. This relationship to being is not new. You can tell an ancient culture's belief about their Being by how they viewed their Gods.

This moving away from dependence on others is the first step toward acquiring enough presence of mind to direct personal immortality. A fortress of spirit is needed. We have to shrug off inhibiting beliefs that have conditioned us to a herd-type mentality. Antinomian acts and thoughts help condition the will to be able to violate natural laws by un-conditioning our beliefs about reality. They are a key element in the practice of the Left Hand Path. I refer again to the words of Black and Dr. Hyatt, "...let us say that politics addresses the issue of whether or not you are property or a 'free' man. The area on which this book focuses is the realm of the spiritual. Are you the property of some God or are you a 'free' man? (pg13). Will you become some lackey to feed the ego of some entity, or will you raise yourself to the zenith of individual power (DAIS)?

Right Hand Path

The idea of a Right and Left-Hand Path stems from Indian roots in Hinduism. There is a division within Tantric sects whereby the normal path of energy flow to the right is reversed. It is an intentional breaking out of patterned behavior and belief. The little known Left-Hand-Path has received more and more attention over the past couple decades although the idea is millennia old. The right-hand and left-hand concepts can now be used to classify all religious/philosophical thoughts by their aim.

The Right Hand Path is distinguished by a desire to merge one's Self with God, the Universe, an OverSoul, Cosmic Consciousness, etc... Almost all orthodox (monotheistic) religions project this end for their followers. The modern interpretations of most major religions and their philosophies will clearly point to a belief in the unity of man with god. We are all one, god is everything, everything is god, all beings came from god and all things strive to return to god. Upon death of the individual, their Self is overwhelmed by the presence of another more powerful entity or dissolved entirely.

The Right Hand Path idea leads to another paradoxical dichotomy, that of an all-powerful good god and his evil wretched adversary. Arthur Lyons spells it out for us in *Satan Wants You* saying,

> "All those religious systems in which Satan has appeared share one common trait: they are all monotheistic and, as such, need a negative balance for the positive construct of an all-powerful, all-good, and merciful God. Satan is necessary because there is no other way to dispose of the evil realities constantly confronting humanity. Since pestilence, famine, and death are formidable evils faced by all men, and since it is difficult, to say the least, to attribute their origin to pure goodness, an evil source must be assumed to exist." (20)

The moral and ethical ambiguities that arise out of this titanic battle are mind boggling to say the least. They are so contrary to man's natural proclivities as to make it a wonder of wonders how they survived this long. When faced with the realities of man and the universe it makes absolutely no sense to believe in god/satan. If god is omnipotent and omni-benevolent then evil would not and could not exist. There is no way to resolve this contradiction. The adversary was created to satisfy the problem inherent in supremacy religions that try to be the only One. They also manage to puff themselves up by having a powerful (albeit invisible, illusory) enemy.

Even what is normally thought of in common reincarnation circles has this same Right Hand Path merging. Imagine living the last cycle of life and upon death your current individual self blends with the memories and experiences of 400 other lives each with its own personality (tens of thousands of years of life, millions of conversations, and billions of experiential moments). Where does your current unique identity go in such a case? It is easy to see the obliteration of the Self under these circumstances and a merging with something 'other', even if this 'other' was some version of you.

Man did not always see the Universe in this fashion and he is not confined to those visions now. Many ancient teachings point to a way of the Left Hand Path as not only a valid methodology but also an even more desirable aim.

Left Hand Path

The Left Hand Path is the term used for a methodology and philosophy counter to the destruction of Self. Modern thinkers and practitioners define the Left-Hand Path as the quest for personal ascension and have adopted its name. It is concerned with the preservation of the individual ego. This life has evolved a unique isolate intelligence (Self/Soul) that is worthy of continuation and personal immortality fulfills this very purpose. Dr. Stephen E. Flowers defines it in *Lords of the Left Hand Path* thusly:

> "The left-hand path considers the position of humanity as it is; it takes into account the manifest and deep-seated desire of each human being to be a free, empowered, independent actor within his or her world. The pleasure and pain made possible by independent existence are seen as something to be embraced and as the most reasonable signs of the highest, most noble destiny possible for humans to attain - a kind of independent existence on a level usually thought of as divine." (13)

The Left Hand Path has been associated with evil by persons unfamiliar with its tenants or disturbed by its methods. Their main problem is the fact that followers of the LHP wish to stand outside society and go against their cultural conditioning. Anton Szandor LaVey was the first to bring this ancient path to light (or darkness as it were) in the popular modern world by proclaiming in *The Devil's Notebook*:

> "My brand of Satanism is the ultimate conscious alternative to herd mentality and institutionalized thought. It is a studied and contrived set of principles and exercises designed to liberate individuals form a contagion of mindlessness that destroys innovation." (9)

Where the Right Hand Path teaches denial of the self in this life and a denial/dissolution of Self in the afterlife, the Left-Hand Path views life as the crucible necessary for all Self-development. It embraces the true nature of man (strife, happiness, and freedom) and his experience in the material dimension. In fact, it is this "living" that produces the possibility of Self-realization in the first place.

If you are new to the path you must realize that the road is difficult and fraught with pitfalls; but take heart in knowing that you are not only saving yourself but you are setting an example for others to follow. As Ouspensky says in *Tertium Organum* "It becomes increasingly clear that changes in the external life, i.e. changes in the life of the many, if they must come at all, will come *as a result* of inner changes in the few." (278). If you are a current practitioner of the Left Hand Path you will be rewarded with newfound understanding on your divine quest. The Dark Arts are the toolbox of transformation for the Left-Hand Path practitioner. Regardless of the branch you follow these arts are designed with the methods and goal of the Left Hand Path in mind (antinomianism and Self-deification). The Dark Arts of Immortality lead to a Divinely Ascended Immortal Soul.

Antinomianism

The term antinomianism comes from the Latin *anti-* meaning 'against' and the Greek *nomos* meaning law. So it literally means the practice of doing something "against the law". Webster's Dictionary defines antinomian as "2.) One who rejects a socially established morality." It is the practice of going against traditionally held cultural or societal norms. Nietzsche guides us by saying "My insight: all the forces and drives by virtue of which life and growth exist lie under the ban of morality: morality as the instinct to deny life. One must destroy morality if one is to liberate life." (189). It is a necessary practice of the Left Hand Path to decide what is best for one's self so as to liberate one's Self.

In order to strengthen the Self to a point where it can sustain ultimate freedom the will must be tempered like steel. The way to do that is to prove to your self the rules and laws we obey may not be as concrete and universal as once thought. Don't get the idea that you must break all the rules and do just the opposite of everyone else. That would be ludicrous. The idea is to decide for one's self in a rational way the best course of action to attain your personal aims.

Choosing to be anti-cultural or anti-social would be submitting to a form of control and herd conditioning as well. You would fall into the same 'pattern', albeit the opposite pattern, by modeling yourself this way. Instead, choose which of societies rules, virtues, and vices fit your needs and desires and then formulate a plan of your own to utilize these characteristics. By doing this you are free to incorporate or eliminate any quality you wish as they are evaluated for usefulness. You are not fixed by someone else's ideals. You can be flexible, adaptable, and inexorable.

The first experience of freedom is often shocking. It typically occurs in childhood when we have very little control over our own choices. We are constantly told to do something or, more often, not to do things. It is presented to us as incontrovertible. Later in life we discover these hindrances were just for our protection or a method of control used by authority figures. We learn that, in fact, they are controvertible. Those laws and rules are supposed to be discarded when they no longer serve our needs or our best interest. In time some of these notions are rejected to our benefit. Most people hold on to inhibiting childish beliefs long after reaching adulthood and some never rebel against them at all; but we are not concerned here with childhood restrictions.

Each of us carries around other beliefs picked up much later in life from friends, family, and society at large that hinder us in the same way (remember the section on memes). There was a time when no man could run a mile in under four minutes. It was believed to be a physical impossibility. Now even amateur athletes beat that time. Someone had to believe and strive for it regardless of what everyone else thought. Once broken the belief loses the power to restrain that it held before. Unfortunately many people go through life holding on to useless doctrines, most of which are still used by men to control other men. By practicing antinomian techniques one can break the chains of bondage and free the psyche. The memes that have hold on us are powerful but they are not indestructible. Their popularity is not a sure indicator of truth as Bloom points out,

> "...the measure of the success of a web of memes - a myth, a hypothesis, or a dogma - is not its truth but how well it serves as social glue. If a belief system performs that function well enough, it can trigger the growth of a superorganism of massive size, even if its most basic tents prove dead wrong." (108)

The importance of belief cannot be over emphasized. In fact many paths will converge on this one pivotal word. Belief adds conviction to actions, speech, and will. William James agrees by emphasizing:

> "Thought in movement has for its only conceivable motive the attainment of belief, or thought at rest. Only when our thought about a subject has found its rest in belief can our action on the subject firmly and safely begin. Beliefs, in short, are rules for action; and the whole function of thinking is but one step in the productions of active habits." (pg369)

It also filters all perceptions. It defends ideas. It powers self-transformation. It is necessary to overcome your current restrictions. If you hold beliefs about limitations you will be less likely to exceed those limits. As Sarah E. Worth says in her essay *The Paradox of Real Response to Neo-Fiction*:

> "Our knowledge of what is real and what isn't real doesn't necessarily change the way we behave or respond to these things. We may have to face the possibility that the line that divides appearance and reality (in the Matrix and in our own lives) is not as clear as we once though it to be. We may even need to actively make that line disappear in order to make sense of our interactions with fictions."[2]

I am not saying to abandon all principles upon which you base your life. I am suggesting that you pay more attention to the beliefs you cling to and make sure they serve your purposes and are not preventing you from achieving your greatest desires. As Huston Smith put it when speaking of the value we place on science:

> "Though man's conversion to the scientific outlook is understandable psychologically, logically it involves a clean mistake. Insofar as we allow our minds to be guided by reason, we can see that to try to live within the scientific view of reality would be like living in a house's scaffolding, and to love it like embracing one's spouse's skeleton."

(pg8)

Our current non-scientific beliefs may be like that same 'skeleton.' You need to constantly evaluate those beliefs, rebuild the ones that are of further use, and discard those that no longer serve you. Seek the whole of existence not just a piece of it.

Sometimes we fear change and the difficulties involved in coming to grips with the new process so we avoid it at all cost. So resistant are we to change that we will tolerate any pain that is tolerable to avoid it. Don't let it hold you back. Peter J. Carroll in *Liber Chaos* explains,

> "A curious error has entered into many systems of occult thought. This is the notion of some higher self or true will which has been misappropriated from the monotheistic religions. There are many that like to think they have some inner self, which is somehow more real or spiritual than their ordinary or lower self. The facts do not bear this out. There is no part of one's beliefs about one's self which cannot be modified by sufficiently powerful psychological

---

[2] *Ibid* (185)

techniques. There is nothing about one's self which cannot be taken away or changed. The proper stimuli can, if correctly applied, turn communists into fascists, saints into devils, the meek into heroes, and vice-versa. There is no sovereign sanctuary within our selves which represents our real nature. There is nobody at home in the internal fortress. Everything we cherish as our ego, everything we believe in, is just what we have cobbled together out of the accident of our birth and subsequent experiences." (164)

And make no mistake about it. If you do not take active control of those changes someone else will. Someone will take it upon himself or herself to tell you how to think and what to believe. In fact, they already have.

Our ancestors understood this long ago and tried to hand down these secrets in their myths of their Gods/esses and legends of their heroes. Odin is an intimidating figure in all of Germanic folklore and mythology. He constantly encourages his chosen heroes to commit acts against society in order to receive longevity. The crimes spoken of here are the need for the hero to commit acts of rebellion against the three divisions of society; sovereignty, force, and fecundity. This step is paramount to the development of an empowered Being and will be required in the practice of the Dark Arts in order to attain DAIS.

Self-Deification

Quite simply the goal of the Left Hand Path is ascension to godhood. It is the transformation into a self-aware, individual, enlightened, immortal, semi-divine entity. For the path of the Dark Arts we use the term Divinely Ascended Immortal Soul (DAIS).

Every individual has within the cells the code for biological development (DNA). Man contains a similar blueprint within the mind and spirit for development of consciousness and Being. Leibnitz put forth the idea their was a soul monad (particle, unit of force). He believed its nature moved it toward self-realization of its own volition. This was an intrinsic part of the psyche. Body composition is influenced by our environment and experiences, so too is our pattern for consciousness and spiritual growth. Just as someone can waste physical and mental potential through laziness and ignorance, so too can spiritual growth potential be squandered. In other words, the programming necessary to achieve a divine nature is contained in the individual but it is up to you to utilize that potential.

The primary method of educating and conditioning the Self to be able to achieve divine status is through the practice of the dark arts of war, sex, and magic. As Don Webb so eloquently states in describing forms of knowing,

> "The third technique, noetic inspiration, takes you to the discovery of your own divinity and the edge of Black Magic. We take the term *noesis* from Plato. Plato defined three types of knowing. The lowest is *pistis* (faith). This means believing something because someone in authority tells you so... The next higher way of knowing is *dianoia* (reasoning)...the test of reason and logic... The highest knowing is *noesis* - direct knowledge. This is the knowing that comes from the divine Self." (111)

In actuality there really is no distinction between white and black magic. Humans have a terrible habit of trying to classify everything into nice little categories, especially to make taboo concepts more palatable. Magic, as defined in the first chapter, is a methodology whereby the will, guided by belief, augments or violates causality in conformance to one's intent. It is clear from this definition that the power comes from within the magician. It does not matter the nature of the work being performed so to separate it in to terms of black and white is useless.It is for aesthetic appeal and antinomian value we keep the term Black Magic alive and well.

Magic used to be a religious practice that raised pneuma within the individual. It is the source of the power that really distinguishes it from other technologies such as prayer. With prayer comes the practice of handing off control and responsibility to some other power in the hope that things will turn out ok. This is the same habit people have of not evaluating their own beliefs and the memes they are bound by. William James agrees that invisible forces help make things happen and says: "Through prayer, religion insists, things which cannot be realized in any other manner come about: energy which but for prayer would be bound is by prayer set free and operates in some part, be it objective or subjective, of the world of facts." (386). The difference is that here people are subverting their own will and power and allowing some other entity to control the outcome. This can be a problem in several ways. There is the distinct possibility that no entity exists to take care of it, so they are using a weakened version of their own will (wishful thinking). While it can result in a certain piece of mind there is no personal development. If there is some entity willing to change things it may not do it in line with your wishes or best interest. Lastly, the person will tend to do nothing (not act, speak or will) after praying which reduces the possibility of the event occurring.

The handicap of these beliefs is accountability. Giving up control of one's life results in excuses for poor results.

Magic typifies the whole concept of the LHP as it is a "take charge" attitude requiring extraordinary work and effort. Consider it the equivalent to exercise for the body, and education for the mind. Magic is necessary for the practitioner of the Left-Hand-Path to be able to gain real mastery over their Self. It is the mastery of desire and the drives of Man that will prevent the waste of spiritual potential. Don't worry if you have never practiced magic before. You are quite capable of practicing black magic because just as Bloom explains when speaking of psychological factors, "In humans, however, the personalities that could have been are always there, always uncomfortable in their imprisonment. And periodically they scream from the dungeons of the mind, demanding their freedom." (94). Now we have taken your powers out of the darkness and the dungeon gates are thrown wide. So get to work!

The Dark Arts of Immortality are designed to maximize physical, mental, and spiritual actualization in the pursuit of a more complete left-hand path methodology. They exceed the mere use of magic as the single most important aspect by adding sex and war and the dark arts fill in some gaps that have been missing (namely the altered states of being and consciousness). The Dark Arts of Immortality complete the antinomian triad of practices necessary to pursue self-deification (DAIS).

Blazing a Black Trail

The evil-ution of thought from the oldest philosophies to the modern path of darkness has been a long one. Man has spent so much time and energy in his advancement of technology he has ignored himself. But now that the tide is turning it is up to us to keep up the momentum.

As *Friedrich Nietzsche says*, "The *philosopher* as a further development of the priestly type: - has the heritage of the priest in his blood; is compelled, even as rival, to struggle for the same ends with the same means as the priest of his time; he aspires to supreme authority." (89). It is from these words that we will look at some of the philosophers that contributed to the aspiration of 'supreme authority'.

One of the greatest quests in the history of Man was the alchemical quest for the Philosophers stone. Alchemy was about the process of transforming one substance into another. The idea of turning lead into gold was just a metaphor for changing the state of existence of a human being into a spiritual Being. It was not about external materials, it was about internal processes.

The way to the Philosophers stone is through libido, mortido, and physis. The human drives in the greatest strength that can be endured will lead the way to immortality and a powerful existence in the here and now. The transformation of lead into gold takes place inside the human Being.

Aristotle would have agreed with the idea of a Left Hand Path. For him self-realization was the highest aim for Man. It was a way to gage all other actions and regardless of what those actions entailed if they took one closer to the aim it was considered good. We will modify this usage of good with the term right. Good will reflect intent not results.

According to Frost:

> "Kierkegaard evolved a philosophical system which divided existence into three categories; that is, he claimed that experience may be of three kinds: aesthetic, ethical, and religious. The child is an example of the individual who lives almost exclusively at the aesthetic level. For the child, all choices are made in terms of pleasure and pain, and experience is ephemeral, having no continuity, no meaning, but being merely a connection of isolated, non-related moments. The ethical level of experience involves choice; whenever conscious choice is made, one lives at the ethical level. At the religious level one experiences a commitment to oneself, and an awareness of one's uniqueness and singleness. To live at the religious level means to make any sacrifice, any antisocial gesture that is required by being true to oneself. Clearly, these levels are not entirely separable, but may coexist." (264)

Modern pioneers of the Left Hand Path are the late Anton Szandor LaVey, Dr. Michael Aquino, Don Webb, and Dr. Stephen E. Flowers. While LaVey would get credit for being the harbinger of darkness it would pass to Dr. Michael Aquino as the master of refining that darkness into a useful process for self-development. Aquino's approach divided the universe into the natural order, philosophic thought, and magical reality. He believed that individuals had psychic and spiritual existence that transcended the more mundane level of the material world.

Left Hand Path schools and religious organizations are the only ones dedicated to advancing this knowledge and giving access to its secrets. Among them are the Church of Satan, the Temple of Set, the Rune-gild, and DAIS.

Evil & Good

The Universe is what it is: it is a system of cause and effect. The waves in the ocean of events do not avoid certain shores because they are 'good.' They wash over them all just the same. Bloom puts it this way:

> "At its heart, the Lucifer Principle looks something like this: The nature scientists uncover has crafted our viler impulses into us: in fact, these impulses are a part of the process she uses to create. Lucifer is the dark side of cosmic fecundity, the cutting blade of the sculptor's knife. Nature does not abhor evil; she embraces it. She uses it to build. With it, she moves the human world to greater heights of organization, intricacy and power." (pg2)

Since it appears nature is attempting to realize itself by evolving then we could argue, as Aristotle would, that these things are actually good since they move it closer to its aim. Since they are part of our nature the same truth applies. Bloom goes on to recognize this very fact when he says,

> "Evil is a by-product, a component, of creation. In a world evolving into ever-higher forms, hatred, violence, aggression, and war are part of the evolutionary plan. ...Superorganism [according to him this includes war], ideas, and the pecking order - these are the primary forces behind much of human creativity and earthly good. They are the holy trinity of the Lucifer Principle." (2 and 326)

The idea that the universe is a battle between good and evil is a useless crutch that must be disposed of. For too long it has been used as the reason why bad things happen to good people and an excuse for people who perform wrong acts in the name of goodness. It is far too easy for people to blame someone else for the problems of the world, and far too easy to shift accountability to someone or something else. This loss of individual accountability must be corrected. You are responsible for the things you do, say, and will and also for the things you don't do, say, and will. Only you! That being said, you must also understand that every act has evil and good consequences. In fact, each person's very existence is both evil and good. In order for a person to eat a delicious meal something must die (plant, animal, etc.). Of course nowadays these killings take place behind closed doors out of the sight of the delicate sensibilities of civilized society. Of course, this causes a misguided use of mortido (death drive) as mentioned earlier. Even driving to visit a sick loved one could be classified as an evil act once you admit the fact that it causes pollution of the atmosphere. Face it: every material possession a person acquires comes at the expense of someone or something else. Adding a little Nietzschean logic here seems appropriate "If therefore an action can be evaluated neither by its origin, nor by its consequences, nor by its epiphenomena, then its value is "x," unknown." (165). We cannot speak clearly about something with an unknown value. Further problems arise when using a word that has several conflicting definitions or means one thing to one group and something entirely different to another. We must un-tangle the concepts of right and wrong with good and evil. To hit the mark we must also clarify consequences and intent within these definitions. The divisions must be distinct so the crossover makes sense.

For clarity it is necessary to separate right and wrong from evil and good. Regardless of the consequences of an action, it can only be deemed evil or good based on the belief and intent of the one performing it. For every action or word used there is an outcome. It may be as simple as taking a drink of water to quench thirst, or speaking a phone number to someone to convey information. The outcome, though, depends on many factors. Intent is the outcome desired and aimed for by the action taken or word spoken. A good action would be one in which the person acted based on what they thought was true at the time, and their intent took into consideration minimizing the adverse affects to everyone and everything else. The determining factor of evil and good is intent and can only be made at the moment of choice and only with knowledge of the mind of the individual performing it. In all times and places one man's evil was another man's good.

For the purpose of this work, right will be defined as those actions or choices that bring one closer to Self-realization and wrong as those moving one away from that attainment. Of course, it may only be possible to evaluate these in hindsight. Unlike evil and good, which are judged only at the instant of choice via intent, right and wrong can only be judged after its effects have been determined. In this way the separation of evil and good from right and wrong will be easily understood. It also allows for some unusual pairings (i.e. evil right action, good wrong action). Just as the Material dimension uses 'evil' for its own growth so too can man harness evil for a noble purpose. Sometime in your life it will be the right thing to do something evil and the wrong thing to do something good. Maybe it already happened. Now you can be comfortable in the knowledge.

This should be liberating information in the sense that it alleviates unnecessary feelings of guilt from the individual. Enjoyment of this should follow as Peter J. Carroll says in *Liber Null & Psychonaut*, "The solution is to become omnivorous. Someone who can think, believe, or do any of a half dozen different things is more free and liberated than someone confined to only one activity." (45). It also comes with great responsibility. You can no longer blame the world for your problems. It is not out to get you through some karmic retribution. It is obvious if you treat someone poorly either that individual or someone who knows about those actions will be inclined to treat you in a like manner. To think that the universe will spank a person because of his or her behavior is ridiculous.

As we have seen this 'evil' is a natural part of the Universe and as Nietzsche thankfully states

> "I assess the power of a will by how much resistance, pain, torture it endures and knows how to turn to its advantage; I do not account the evil and painful character of existence a reproach to it, but hope rather that it will one day be more evil and painful than hitherto." (pg206)

Without this 'evil' we would be nothing and achieve nothing.

V. Divine Paradigm

*True godlessness is not the absence of gods,
but a state in which their presence or absence
makes no difference to us.*

-Heidegger

When we read the myths of our ancestors we can view them in four primary ways. The stories can be read as pure fairy tale fiction, they can be taken literally, they could be accepted as a direct communication from the Gods/esses, or as a primitive way to pass on wisdom. It would be impossible to read every myth and classify them all under one of the above categories. The way to approach the problem is to find a preeminence of myth or a pattern of information that is repeated. This should indicate the importance placed on them and gives an indicator as to where to start the search.

I submit that the first two can be eliminated relatively quickly. When reading with the combination of a critical eye and open mind they reveal themselves. The myths are not written and were not told to others strictly as stories of entertainment. It was initially a way to store and pass on information. If we take them literally it would mean the stories are accurate representations of the interaction of Man and the Gods/esses. That Gods/esses have walked the earth and interacted with men. The lessons learned in this case would tell us how to live in concert with the higher powers. Since we have no current powers walking among us this would seem a waste of time at this point.

The remaining two categories seem more plausible.

Looked at as a direct communication from the Gods/esses would basically mean men wrote the works after a direct inspiration from the Gods/esses. Considering what we understand of the Universe, it seems possible they transmitted messages to individuals here in the Material dimension through the astral (subjective) and ethereal (noujective) links. Especially if you accept the idea they somehow created us you would certainly think they had the ability to communicate valuable information. You would also think they are interested in our benefit and therefore we should listen to them. This certainly solves the conditions according to William James when he says,

> "Meanwhile the practical needs and experiences of religion seem to me sufficiently met by the belief that beyond each man and in a fashion continuous with him there exists a larger power which is friendly to him and to his ideals. All that the facts require is that the power should be both other and larger than our conscious selves." (432)

The Germanic myths seem to satisfy both cases, and are especially appealing since they contain lessons for our ascension.

If we read them as informative stories that pass on ancient wisdom, we must take them seriously. Primitive man was much closer to his natural self and spirit than we are today despite our righteous indignation. The myths are not meant to define the divine but only give an indication of its nature. We might use Eskimos as an example. Where a modern city dwelling denizen may have a few words to describe the color of snow the Eskimos have dozens. They are much more aware of white variation because of the amount of exposure to and their intimate familiarity with snow. Our ancestors were much closer to nature and their own natural existence than we. We are distracted by all the communications (thought, talking, news, advertising) going on in the subjective world, and so separated from nature (objective world) by technology it is nearly impossible to duplicate that intimacy with the material order. Philosophy is another good example. Our current philosophers have been unable to divest themselves from the teachings of those 2000 years ago and they answer the same root questions seemingly little to no better. So while our technology has improved many times over in the last two millennia, we have not. It could be argued that we live longer (probably unsuccessfully since it can be shown otherwise) but that is due to living conditions not due to improved Being. Most all other instances you might argue in favor of will not match the exponential increase in technology.

When the Germanic myths are boiled down to their core truths two groups stand out, the myths of the Goddess Freya and those of the God Odin. They are the myths most important to the Germanic peoples. They were the deities of highest importance to our ancestors and when examined they reveal great wisdom that is both informative and aesthetically pleasing. As Dr. Hyatt and Black suggest, "Each person must decide, if they can, what spirits or gods serve his particular desires and destiny and, if they be so inclined, ally themselves with them." (19). Neither of them started their divine state as the head of the pantheon but as time progressed they both achieved that status through their use of the Dark Arts.

Myth vs. History

It is dangerous ground to attempt to cover when one delves into mythology. Figal warns, "A thinking [hermeneutic] that aspires to intimate like myth should not challenge the abyss which separates it from *mythos*. It can speak *like mythos* only by not attempting to speak *as mythos*." (156). We will not attempt to 'challenge the abyss,' but only allow a few readers to peer into the darkness of that abyss.

Most people would argue that history is more factual than mythology. But upon closer examination the case could be made that mythology is closer to truth than history. The victor typically records history. If the enemy is completely vanquished, then only one side of the issue is available. Obviously it is going to carry a moral, ethical, and factual bias toward the victor's culture and values, which is usually evident even without assumption. If there are victorious allies, the accounts done by multiple parties will vary in "factual" data. This occurs in all ages of recoded history. Assuming the loser survives, then we compound the problem. The loser will have an entirely different account of the events as they transpired. If we have multiple allies on the losing side then the problem grows exponentially. It becomes virtually impossible to verify the facts. Over time these "facts" change in light of new evidence or theories. So what is the truth? Which accounts (facts) are correct?

Mythology, on the other hand, is meant to convey wisdom and knowledge. It is not meant to convince someone outside of the culture to another point of view. It is only meant as a record of previous learning and beliefs. Most myths will go unchanged for thousands of years. If they do change it will be at a much slower pace than history, and they will remain closer to the earliest version than say accounts of WWII a hundred years later.

The myths our ancestors passed down are a direct expression of their facts and knowledge. How they understood their Gods, and their own place in the world is related in the stories and legends they produced. The great mythmakers of our time know that to discard them as un-factual or as mere fairy tales would be an injustice. Only by listening to this ancient mythic voice will we be able to find our way again and seal the schism in our psyche between the warrior, lover, and magus. It would be a detriment to the future of all mankind to let this knowledge die.

Odin's Myths

In the Norse (Germanic) cosmology the gods are divided into two groups: the Aesir and Vanir. Odin was the leader of the Aesir.

In the beginning Odin (inspiration) was born along with two brothers (or hypostases) Vili (will), Ve (sacrality). Another name for Odin and his brothers according to Snorri are Har (high or exalted), Hrafnhar (just as high) and third. Their first act was to war with the giant Ymir and through his destruction create the material world of Midgard (Middle-world). The second act of war was between the pantheons of the Aesir gods and the Vanir gods and started because of an incident involving Odin and Freya (see below).

Throughout Odin's myths is the underlying foundation of a thirst for knowledge and seeking of the hidden. In a personal act of magic in his quest for knowledge and power he wounded himself with a spear and hung himself from the world tree for nine nights. He did not eat or drink for nine nights. There he discovered the runes (secrets). As we shall see this is an archetypal use of magic. It includes the use of pain to heighten consciousness. It is clear he did not shut out the pain or separate from his body because he declares, "I took them wailing". The spilling of blood and body suspension are also useful devices. Since he hangs from the world tree, the axis of the universe from which all things emerge, he is outside the effects of causality. In a similar act of sacrifice he removes one of his eyes in exchange for a drink from the well of wisdom. It could symbolize the pain suffered through experience to gain knowledge or the literal pain from an act of magic similar to the tree story. There was little Odin would not sacrifice to succeed in his quest.

In another story a magical drink was created from spittle stolen from the truce ceremony of the second war, and mixed with gods'-blood. In retrieving it Odin uses all three of the Dark Arts (war, sex, and magic) and the 'sins' of Dumezil (transgressing fecundity, force, and sovereignty). He uses trickery instead of martial skill to defeat nine armed opponents. He uses magic to shape-change into a snake allowing him to penetrate defenses. He seduces and beds Gunnlod for three nights in exchange for a drink of the mead (magical drink). After consuming the mead contained in three bowls (odhroerir, bodn, and son meaning inspiration, sacred enclosure, and blood) he shape-changes again and makes off with the drink. This mead gives the power of poetry and artistic inspiration and a taste of it is spilled for man. Later Odin, Hoenir, and Lodhur (in some versions it is Loki not Lodhur and in some it is Vili and Ve instead of Hoenir, and Lodhur) create man and woman, Ask and Embla. They give them soul, sense, and being respectively.

Odin is constantly challenging his knowledge against wise beings and always uses his guile to outwit his enemies. In both Voluspa and Baldrs draumar he raises a dead seeress to prophesy. In Grimnismal he survives burning and starvation and causes an attacker to fall on his own sword. In order to gain vengeance for the slaying of his son, Odin seduces and sleeps with Rind, bearing Vali.

Freya's Myths

In the beginning Freya leader of the Vanir came to the Aesir gods in the guise of Gullveig (lust for gold, or gold thirsty). Because of some supposed slight a conflict ensued. The Aesir struck her with spears and burned her in flames. She emerged from the fire unharmed. Three times she was thus attacked and reborn. Edred Thorsson in *Witchdom of the True* identifies this as, "She [Freya] is the one who came of her own fee will and underwent the ordeals of the Aesir and was not destroyed, but rather was transformed, by them." (50). Afterwards she was given the name Heith (shining one) a name often given to witches. War between the Aesir and Vanir raged with neither defeating the other. In the truce that followed Freya came to the Aesir in a hostage exchange. As with Odin she is ever on a quest and although she looks for her lost husband Odur (ecstatic power) it is clear she seeks a mystery of her own. Thorsson adds "It appears that this search for Odhr is an unending one for the Lady [Freya] - but that in her travels she always gains in power and extends her rulership." (54).

She has many names, one of which is Valfreya and survives due to her association with the Valkyrie (choosers of the slain). They are depicted as sky riders who descend onto the battlefield and choose which dead heroes arise to the warrior's paradise. She is said to lead the female warriors into battle. In another myth she is said to select from among the dead champions to reside in her hall (Folkvangr). During the times of her worship she was often envisioned wearing armor and bearing weapons. It is only later that she is depicted as a demon on Valpurgisnacht (Witches Night).

Freya was said to be a great witch and even taught her type of sorcery to Odin who was already a master of his own brand of magic. It was said that this was woman's magic, which could allude to sex-magic practices some of which we shall cover later. Freya wore Brisingamen (the necklace of the Brisings). In obtaining the necklace she had to sleep successively with the four dwarfs who created it. It is stolen from her and to achieve its return she must promise to cause war and strife between two kings. The battle that ensues is called the Hjadningavig and is similar to the battles in Valhalla wherein the warriors arise after being slain to continue fighting (this could reflect the myths of Folkvangr being a mirror image of Valhalla). In Thrymskvida she conveys the ability to fly to Loki, and in another myth she refuses to marry a giant in exchange for the return of Thor's hammer but helps him retrieve it by giving him her likeness and necklace. Her myths, like Odin's, carry the brand of the Dark Arts and the 'sins' of Dumezil.

Dumezil's Divisions and Sins

In his work on the divisions within the Indo-European culture Georges Dumezil speaks of three distinct classes. The divisions are producer, warrior, and priest-king and their functions are fecundity, force, and sovereignty. They duplicate Plato's caste suggestion for a utopian society in the Republic (craftsman, warrior, philosopher-king), the Greek being Indo-European as well.

For the Germanic people fecundity was inexorably connected with fertility both in terms of sex and agriculture. The warrior way of force was well represented in all areas because as Tacitus says in *The Agricola and the Germania* "He [the German] thinks it tame and spiritless to accumulate slowly by the sweat of his brow what can be got quickly by the loss of a little blood." (114). They showed great reverence for both magical power and leadership. Usually the chieftain of a tribe or king of the land was the spiritual head as well (sovereignty).

Odin and Freya assumed all three roles through their transcendent practices. They both represent the fertility or production aspect. They also both took on the warrior aspects. Further, they were both magicians, which equates directly to priest/philosopher king. Thorsson explains the process in *Witchdom of the True*:

> "Odhinn as the chief sovereign God of the Germanic peoples is a God who specializes in synthesizing opposites. As such he is an ideal model for an "Imperial God," i.e. one who expands his fields of rulership to take in the realms of other divinities. *Working from above* [position of sovereignty] he becomes a God of warriors, and a God of wealth, pleasure and production... [Freya], not to be outdone, expands her fields of rulership *working from below* [fecundity]. She, as primarily a Goddess of wealth, pleasure and production, takes in a warrior function and comes to be considered a sovereign queen... These two tendencies should not be understood in *historical terms* -

they are intrinsic and innate in the essences of the two divinities." (85)

They are intrinsic in us as well. Remember our discussion of memes and how our culture reflects our nature. The reason the Indo-European culture was separated into these three divisions is because it mimics the three parts of our Selves.

The tripartite nature shows up in many areas of myth. In *Runelore: A Handbook of Esoteric Runology*, Thorsson identifies it for us saying,

> "The essential Odhinic structure is threefold. The oldest name of this tripartite entity is *Wodhanaz-Wiljon-Wihaz* (Odhinn-Vili-Ve). The meanings of these names show us how this tripartite entity of consciousness works. *Wodh-an-az* (master of inspiration {*whodh-*}) is the expansive all-encompassing ecstatic and transformative force at the root of consciousness and enthusiasm. *Wiljon* (the will) is the conscious application of a desired plan consciously arrived at, and *Wihaz* (the sacred) is the spirit of *separation* in an independent sacred "space." ...all three should work together as a whole." (179)

At the very beginning Bor along with Bestla births Odin, Vili, and Ve (inspiration, will, sacrality). Ymir births an entity from under each arm and one at the feet. The mead of inspiration was joined from three vessels (odhroerir, bodn, and son meaning inspiration, sacred vessel, and blood). The nine worlds of Norse cosmology are divided into three realms upper, middle, lower.

Man's very creation was a tripartite event. Man and woman are given three gifts. Depending on the version and translation the three are spirit of life, sharp wits, and sight. or soul, sense, being, or spirit, discernment, and divine light, or life's breath, mind, and body. This obviously reflects and is further proof of a deep-seated belief in spirit, mind, and body. It is very telling that in the myths where Odin creates the elves and dwarfs they were not given this tripartite nature. This is another indication of our uniqueness. We are further developed in the *Lay of Rig*. Man is given the seed of the Gods/esses over three successive generations creating Thrall, Carl, and Jarl. After the improvements are made on these successive generations Kon (meaning king) is born and appears to transcend all three functions. He is instructed to go out and experience life.

At some point this tripartite nature was split. It could have been anywhere in our past. Dudley Young pinpoints it extremely far back identifying "alpha-shaman". Alpha represents both the warrior and fecund and shaman of course represents priest-king. He suggests, "...the splitting of these roles [alpha male and shaman] opened a rift in the human psyche that we have been trying ever since to repair." (148). He is absolutely right in this regard; if we look back we will see this schism in consciousness, in belief, and in being. We have given up these multiple roles to specialization. But the clues are there in our myths and legends waiting for us to return to them. Young adds "...at the mythic center of virtually every culture is the story of the hero, and the hero looks like alpha-shaman, who may save both himself and us by refusing to be split in two [three]." (155).

So how do we accomplish this miraculous feat? Through the Dark Arts and the 'sins' of Dumezil. In addition to identifying the three divisions (fecund, warrior, priest-king) of Indo-European culture Georges Dumezil also identifies the antinomian triad of the myths and legends. As Rick Fields says in *Code of the Warrior*, "Dumezil's distinctive Indo-European warrior-hero is a volatile and stormy figure who represents an opposition inherent in the very structure of Indo-European society." (66). This 'opposition' is shown in the actions of the hero when he violates the dictates of each cultural division. The hero rebels against the rules of each class. He usually disobeys or kills a ruler or priest, acts out of lust or deceit against a producer, and uses trickery to defeat an opponent instead of martial skill.

Dumezil also points out the idea that the hero, if he is to be successful must take on aspects of the enemy he is fighting. He must become like the very evil he is fighting against. In fact it could be said that the greater the villain the more society benefits. The hero will need to grow more powerful in order to rescue society and therefore reaches greater heights than he would have ordinarily. It is certainly the case that the more dangerous the opponent, the more powerful the hero (or anti-hero) must become in order to defeat him. By that reasoning, he takes on more of the villainous nature of 'evil' or 'other' to raise his own power. That knowledge is then reintegrated into the society he protects and hence elevates the entire culture.

After all of these transgressions he goes through a sort of transformative process (rebirth), possibly to assimilate his newly acquired powers. This matches the heroic process described by Dr. Flowers as separation (he breaks the rules of society), transformation (he becomes something 'other'), and re-inclusion (he assimilates the new abilities and returns). Now that we have identified the process for the hero it should be clear it is reflected in the myths. The actions of the Gods/esses match this very same change and the myth of the Ragnarok (Twilight of the Gods) may be a phase of transformation for the Gods/esses.

Here we begin to get a glimpse of the Dark Arts of war, sex, and magic. In the myths of both Odin and Freya they use them repeatedly to solve problems and advance their quest. The reason this is so important is because it leads to an understanding of our nature. Since the myth of Ragnarok shows the destruction of some of the Gods/esses it shows the parallel of their attempts to avoid annihilation with our own. In the immortal words of C. G. Jung as heard in this passage from *The Psychology of C. G. Jung* by Jolande Jacobi,

> "'But,' says Jung, 'he who speaks in primordial images speaks with a thousand voices; he enthralls and overpowers, while at the same time he lifts the idea he is trying to express out of the occasional and the transitory into the realm of the ever-enduring. He transmutes our personal destiny into the destiny of mankind, thereby evoking in us all those beneficent forces that have always enabled mankind to find a refuge from every peril and to outlive the longest night.'" (24)

Cult of Odin

One of the most striking and puzzling facts about the worship of Odin is the lack of evidence. Odin was the highest God in the Norse pantheon and yet very few names or place names exist utilizing his name. Even obscure Gods/esses of the pantheon have significantly more personal and geographic representation. Scholars have had difficulty with this but the answer is quite simple. Odin's cult was a secret society. Edred Thorsson tells us why this is so in *Runelore: A Handbook of Esoteric Runology* when he says, "Whereas other religious cults turn outward to the Objective manifestation of the particular god, the cult of Odhinn turns inward and seeks a deification of the Self." (179). This shadow world of his followers had no reason to see the light of day. The trail to its origin has been available to us all along. We will speak of it briefly here and develop it fully in the section on Einherjar and Valkyrie.

The most recent legends related to the worship of Odin stem from the images of the Wild Hunt. It was described as a band of black painted warriors riding through the sky accompanied by a pack of baying black wolves. In *The Cult of Odin* by H. M. Chadwick he references "Golther (Mytholigie, p. 292 ff.) holds that Woden [Odin] is a deified development of Wode, the leader of the ghostly army (*das wutende Heer*) [Wild Hunt] which is supposed to dash through the air on stormy nights." (66). They exhibited powers related to the use of the Dark Arts in their mad dash across Europe. Otto Hofler does an in depth study of the men's bands (warrior bands) or *mannerbund* and their relationship to secret societies. He directly identifies the Wild Hunt as a cult of Odin extending from the ancient Germanic tribe described by Tacitus (Roman historian), called the Harii.

The older evidence we have suggests that the worship of Odin was not a pretty sight. Adam of Bremen states "Woden id est furor". It was not a passive affair. This is of course understandable considering the source of the information. H. R. Ellis-Davidson in *Gods and Myths of Northern Europe* says, "In the earlier days of Germanic heathenism the terrible wholesale slaughter of captured forces and criminals implies a belief in a god of battles who demanded that blood should flow in his honour." (71). Stephen Pollington agrees in *The English Warrior from Earliest Times to 1066* by saying, "In the case of the Norse worship of Odhinn, warfare became an end in itself, virtually a religious act - the greater the number of enemies slain, the more devout the warrior was held to be - and at the same time death in battle ensured a seat in the war-god's hall." (169). Even women got into the act as H. R. Ellis-Davidson explains in *Viking Road to Byzantium*:

> "As to whether the conception of women warriors, also associated with Odin and his heroes, might have originated in the eastern region, the evidence here is inconclusive. Such a tradition was known among the Sarmatians in the third century BC, when girls were said to fight along with men and to be required to slay an enemy before they could be given in marriage." (311)

But these are only visible manifestations of the warrior nature. They lack the full spectrum of transcendent practices. The true heart of the cult of Odin still lies hidden and will remain so until another chapter.

Cult of Freya

> *"Many are those who study the art of the children of darkness, who call themselves by the names of witch and warlock, who gaze at crystals, read the tarot, divine by divers means, and seek success through paths of magic. All these play at the Devil's game and take the Devil's tools in their quest for crumbs of power. In the name of all who suffered and died as the agents of the Devil in ages past, the present band of heretics - those who would deny the Devil, yet play His game - must be called to task."*
> ANTON SZANDOR LAVEY IN THE DEVIL'S NOTEBOOK

You may question my opening this chapter with that quote, but it is quite fitting indeed for Freya is *the witch*. The oldest mention of the witches Sabbath is by Pope Gregory IX in 1234 C. E. In *Nordic Legacy* it says "Odin survived only as a leader of the Wild Hunt in a few regions of Sweden, and Freyja was presented as the witch who led the Sabbath orgies on *Walpurgisnacht* (April 30) in German legend." It was said that witches gathered on a hilltop by the light of the full moon. They arrived either by flying or riding on wolves. Sometimes they rode on man-wolves. Their raucous dancing and sexual orgies lasted through the night. Davidson illuminates other clues in *The Gods and Myths of Northern Europe* with,

> "We know a good deal about *seidhr* from prose sources, and it forms an interesting clue to the nature of her [Freya] cult. ...There is little doubt that there was a darker side to seidhr and all that it represented. ...it is easy to discern two distinct sides of the cult of the goddess... Thus the religion of the Vanir was bound to include orgies, ecstasies, and sacrificial rites." (117)

These prophetesses held many functions that included riding into battle with the armies. They would perform divinations, blood sacrifices, and at times pick up weapons and charge into battle.

The Germans had a long standing belief in women's magical abilities as *Tacitus* shows two thousand years ago "More than this, they believed that there resides in women an element of holiness and a gift of prophecy; and so they do not scorn to ask their advice, or lightly disregard their replies." (108). In addition he points out a connection of the Goddess to a warrior element stating "They worship the Mother of the gods, and wear, as an emblem of this cult, the device of a wild boar, which stands them instead of armour or human protection and gives the worshipper a sense of security even among his enemies." (139). Freya was associated with the boar and is described as riding one into battle. There are also descriptions of women riding with an army urging their men to fight and milling in the field afterwards. Just as the visible elements of the cult of Odin are one-dimensional so too are the visible elements of Freya's cult. The other elements are hidden as well. It is fitting given her lustful nature and myths of sexual manipulation that at least one element survived the misogynistic Dark Ages. We will see a clear connection of the cults of Odin and Freya in the section on Valkyrie and Einherjar.

Form, Idea, Essence

In the philosophy of Plato, form and idea have the same meaning. Later philosophers such as Aristotle and Descartes modified their usages to define whether any form presented to our senses was just a copy while the idea of the object held in the mind was real or visa versa. There was a later disagreement between rationalists and empiricists over whether ideas were present in the mind originally or only gained through experience. At times there was also a blurring of meaning with archetype. It was at once used as an original first form and at times an ideal goal to aim for. It is necessary to clarify these terms in order to utilize the word archetype without confusion.

Similarly to the concepts of wrong and right, evil and good we need to make the terms referring to form and idea useful for the modern reader by defining them properly. Modern textbooks fail to explain the concepts of form and idea in a concise usable manner. Form will refer to the objective manifestation of an item that projects an image, which helps it be identified for what it is. Form includes activities related to abstract concepts such as justice, honor, etc. Idea is the concept suggested by the mind about some thing or held in the mind because of some thing. Essence is the core quality, nature, or potential seeking expression. Forms and ideas can vary widely but the essence tends to unite various versions of a form or idea (i.e. there are many forms of a couch, many ideas of couches, but the essence (key characteristic) is the same and unites them). Archetype is the purist combination of a thing's form, idea, and essence.

Let us make an example using the words form, idea, essence, and archetype. A couch presents itself to an observer in a way that helps the intellect identify it. That is its form, the image it projects. The concept in the mind that allows for identification is the idea of couchness. The qualities that make it a couch to you, its "couchness", are its idea. It can work the other way around as well. In order to create a couch one must have the idea of couchness in the mind. What qualities make a couch a couch? Then it is possible to create its form (an objective something that projects the qualities of couchness which another person could identify). Keep in mind that the form may project one thing and our minds each interpret it slightly differently. What is its particular couchness to me (my mind) may be something different to you (your mind). What each of us sees in our mind's eye when looking at the same couch will be different. Obviously the couch itself (its form) and our perception of it (idea) are different. We can measure the form but how do you measure your idea of it. This shows that form and idea cannot be the same thing. They must be different not only in degree but also in kind (remember the chapter with brain/consciousness and material/astral).

This example seems clear enough until we consider the first couch. Which came first the form or the idea? Could the idea exist in the mind without the first form? Could the form be created without the first idea? Was there some form that reflected couchness to the mind? Or, did the idea of couchness impose itself on matter? The answer to all of these questions could be yes and no.

This is where essence comes in. It is the couchism (state of being) that transcends both the couch and couchness in this way. It is the core potential for actualization of the form and idea and at the same time the key characteristic, which form and idea strive to express. Every object, every virtue, every act has this essence, this potential for manifestation and actualization of its key nature. Essence is also different in kind from form and idea. While forms can vary widely between similar objects and ideas about the same form can vary widely among persons, the essence of like objects is the same. There are thousands of variations of couches (form and idea) but the essence of what a couch is manifesting is the same among all couches (i.e. multiple-sitting).

So now we have essence, form, and idea. Form being the image projected, idea being the qualities interpreted by the mind, and essence being the potential for actualization of a core nature. We have to eliminate the concept of linear time, as we understand it now. We could answer the questions above differently for different things. Again we must begin at the beginning. If initially a stump presented to the mind the quality of sitting and the mind expanded this concept to a multi-sitting object then the idea of a couch could pre-exist the form. If instead there were two people and they sat together on a log, then the essence, multi-sitting (couchism), preexisted the form and idea. But what if a lone individual made a large seat from a log without the concept of sharing it with another individual. Here the essence cannot be actualized because we have only one person so no multi-sitting, but the form exists. Essence cannot be actualized, hence does not exist, until we add another person.

Having clarified the other terms we are ready to understand archetype as the embodiment of form, idea, and essence. It will be the manifestation of a form that actualizes itself by presenting to the mind the idea of its essence. With the archetype of something it will be impossible to take it for anything other than what it is because it manifests all three elements fully and harmonioiusly. For example, someone could see the administration of justice as injustice (i.e. capital punishment). For the archetype of justice it would be so pure that all would recognize it as such. It is only possible through the purist blending of form, idea, and essence. Therefore it is only possible with the first one. Any change in this first archetype is just a copy. It may look prettier, or smell different, or change the original in some way but the original is still closest to the purest combination of its essence with form and idea. If you believe there are ascended beings already we can harness their power by taking ourselves back to the beginning in search of the archetype. We must model our Selves on the oldest successful manifestation possible and at the same time strive for actualizing our unique essence.

Using Socratic thinking some leaps of deduction could be made. Keep in mind that even what we think of as matter is just a type of energy. Everything is energy. Forms exist in our Objective world in the Material dimension. Ideas exist in our Subjective world in the Astral dimension. Essences exist in our Noujective world in the Ethereal dimension. Outside of our limited perception of linear time everything that already exists in the Universe must have form, idea, and essence. Every form must present to the mind the idea of itself, and express a key quality (essence). Every idea must have an expression in form and reveal a core nature. Every essence can be manifested in myriad forms and actualized in various ideas. So all things (except No-thing, which cannot exist) have the potential for actualizing themselves through form recognition, idea conception, or essence manifestation. Therefore, if a form exists there must be the idea and essence of it. If the idea exists there must be a form and essence of it. And if there is an essence of something its idea and form can exist. If it exists, then there is an archetype.

It could be said that a table has the potential for an immortal soul. But a table does not present to the mind the idea of an immortal soul nor does it express immortality as its core nature. So the existence of immortality in a table is unlikely. Man does however present to the mind the idea of an immortal soul. Many creatures have a sentience of sorts (some solve problems, some use tools, and apes have been trained to communicate in sign language, etc.). The distinguishing factor for us is the knowledge of our mortality, hence the invention of religion, and the quest for immortality. Since, Man has Being beyond the simple sentience of animals it can be said the essence of immortality has expression in man through spirit. If there is an idea of it, or there is an essence of it, then there can be a form. This line of thinking does not necessarily prove that an immortal soul currently exists in man. It only proves that the possibility for manifesting immortality exists in man. It is up to us to achieve its actualization. The Dark Arts of Immortality are the path to a Divinely Ascended Immortal Soul.

	Self			
	Body	Mind	Spirit	
Timeframe				**Awareness**
Urd	Lik	Minni	Fylgia	Subconscious
Verdandi	Hamr	Hugr	Hamingja	Conscious
Skuld	Sal	Odr	Ond	Supraconscious
	Objective	Subjective	Noujective	
		Worlds		

Self Complex

VI. Self-Evolution Theory

...in order to become a different Being,
man must want it very much and for a very long time.
A passing desire or vague desire
based on dissatisfaction with external conditions
will not create a sufficient impulse.
                                    -P. D. Ouspensky

In order to understand the theory of self-evolution it may be helpful to have a basic understanding of organic evolution and the correlation between the two. By evolution, I mean the process of development and growth with the acquiring of powers not already possessed. Combining this with a foundation of knowledge about the construction of the Germanic body-mind-soul complex and how it functions within the context of a time element may give some conclusions about guiding self ascension. When we talk about the soul we will be referring to the immortal being we evolve into, a Divinely Ascended Immortal Soul, not a preexisting spirit.

Survival of the Adaptive

Darwin's theory of evolution has been misinterpreted many times and has been used to justify differing points of view. This section is based on the idea that his theory was not survival of the "fittest" but survival of the most "adaptive" (to nature). (Within the modern studies of evolutionary psychology the following truths will hold firm.) For example, when he studied birds on the Galapagos Islands the food sources available to the birds were flowers and plants with long bulbs. This allowed the birds with longer beaks to flourish and made it more difficult for short beaked birds to survive. Since they had no predators on the island they took to the ground. Over generations the surviving birds had developed long beaks and were no longer capable of flight. Is a bird with an oversized beak that can't fly the "fittest" of its species? No, of course not. Is it the most harmonized with its natural environment? In this instance, yes, probably so.

Obviously in this situation the birds had exposure to a very limited environment. Does that change the basic premise? No. Even birds in a richer environment develop in a limited way with properties that would be deadly in another location (i.e. bright plumage). Or they adjust their behavior to changes by moving to a similar environment (i.e. migration). Again they are being conditioned by nature and do not become the "fittest" bird.

So how does this apply to man who has the ability to mold his world to suit his needs and desires? Mankind has been able to create a multitude of time and energy saving devices. Does pushing a button help develop the "fittest" physical being? It is now possible to think with machines and to imagine with video games. Do these tools help develop the "fittest" mental being? Most individuals experience the preponderance of their emotions by watching someone else act them out on TV. Does this help develop the "fittest" spiritual being? Thomas S. Hibbs answers the questions this way in his essay *Notes for Underground: Nihilism and the Matrix* "The Enlightenment commitment to the mastery of nature through technological progress risks the degradation of humanity, just as an imprudent celebration of individual freedom paradoxically courts a homogenization of all mankind."[3]

With all the technological gadgets humans still find themselves harmonizing with the environment. Is this environment of our own making the most conducive to complete body-mind-spirit evolution? Is the situation conducive to the creation of a soul (DAIS)? Has man found himself leaving immortal development in someone else's hands? Has he placated himself to the grace and understanding of another? Is he content to harmonize with the universe and let what happens happen? In other words, has he become a physical couch potato, mental sloth, and spiritual sheep? Heidegger thinks so, "In our search for lived experience, we consume never-ending quantities of entertainment and information. We represent beings and play with our representation of beings. But we never open ourselves up to Being itself." (143)

At least the bird has a valid excuse for its condition. It had no conscious choice. People, on the other hand, have chosen poorly or not chosen at all, which is just as bad. People tend to take the easy path to avoid work or pain seeking only comfort or pleasure and then only superficially. They will tolerate the status quo as long as it is tolerable with no thought of improvement or change. But true consciousness is the factor that can turn things around.

---

[3] *Ibid (155)*

It implies more than just being awake, it means being "Awake". A proactive participant on the Universal stage.

Self-Complex

The Germanic self-complex is made up of nine components: Lik, Hamr, Sal, Minni, Hugr, Odr, Fylgja, Hamingja, and Ond. They are subdivided into groups: Physical- Lik, Hamr, Sal. Mental- Minni, Hugr, Odr. Spiritual- Fylgja, Hamingja, Ond. The order that they are listed is important because there is a certain correlation between the grouping, order, and properties of each one. The nine components are woven together with some overlap in ability and backup function. It is best to operate the right one for the right job. That is the reason for study and experimentation (work).

Lik (body): this is the biological structure of bones, muscles, blood and the genetic memory contained in these cells passed down to you. It is the result of generations of the pairings of your ancestors and contains the biological blueprint for construction of the organism.

Hamr (shape): this is a malleable aspect of the physical complex. It is primarily a lacing of the five senses, nervous system and aura.

Sal (shade): this is the shadow matrix underlying the other physical components. It is the dark core, which is fed by the energy produced from extreme feelings of the lik processed by the hamr.

Minni (memory): this is the ability to remember. It is the warehouse of personal knowledge gained throughout life and a transpersonal storehouse of universal knowledge. It is the faculty capable of storing and retrieving recollections of the past and carries the thought-forms for the construction of consciousness.

Hugr (mind): this is the cognitive function of thought and reason. It is the ability to analyze and assimilate information and come to logical conclusions. It is the intellect's ability to shape solutions to problems.

Odr (inspiration): this is the awareness of higher consciousness and enlightenment. It is the heightened state of awakening reached by the wisdom of the minni being processed through the hugr.

Fylgja (fetch): this is the transmitting complex usually envisioned in the form of an animal, person, or geometric shape. It attaches itself to individuals along familial lines and this entity carries with it all of those lifetimes of observation and the essence for construction of the spirit.

Hamingja (luck): this is the guardian aspect of the spiritual complex. It is sometimes thought of in the shape of a person. This personal power manifests itself in the form of shaping events around the individual and it can be directed by willed projection. This is most commonly experienced as luck, charisma, or willpower. Think of this in terms of that intangible something that the criminal detects in the victim. Or what a woman intuitively knows about a great lover. Our ancestors had a conscious knowledge of this complex.

Ond (spark): this is the divine power invested in man. It is the critical energy link to alternate levels of existence created by orlog of the fylgja being processed through the hamingja. Orlog is related to fate although it changes as choices are made. It seems unavoidable only because a person's wyrd (patterned behavior) is likely to continue along the current line.

Three Norns

Keep in mind that this grouping is not the only available configuration. When examining some of the similarities it is possible to discover other ways of understanding and comparing them. One of the ways in which to compare them is within the Germanic concept of time. This concept is embodied in the three Norns: Urd-Verdandi-Skuld. Their names mean That Which Has Become, That Which Is Becoming, and That Which Ought Become respectively. This is not quite the same as Past-Present-Future in the way it is typically understood. It basically means that the events that have occurred in the past (orlog) have an effect on the probable choice (wyrd) being made at this point of change and should result in a foreseeable outcome. When considering the individual this becomes quite clear. Most people tend to build up habits throughout life and continue making the same choices resulting in a predictable pattern of behavior. This idea can be applied on a macroscopic scale to historical events as well. This does not pose a problem if the outcome is a desirable one.

Harmonizing with time can have an effect similar to harmonizing with nature. The bird follows the natural flow of time so its actions are based strictly on genetic coding and environmental events that have led to this point in time. Its actions are habitual and the outcome predictable because it cannot exercise its will to do otherwise. And since we know nature is not entirely looking out for the bird's best interest, it does not become the "fittest" or even the "fitter". Man has fallen into the same trap by his own laziness. He goes along with the normal flow so his "that which ought become" is being predetermined in the same degenerative way. This is not only a detriment to the individual in the short term but also to the species in the long term. It is the difference between being and Being.

The lik-minni-fylgja triad best represents the Urd portion of this comparison. This is the well of wyrd from which we all drink and in turn replenish. It is built up of layer upon layer of "that which has become" since the beginning of time. The past can be available for use by the individual through cellular memory, personal experience, or a connection to ancestral perceptions. It is possible that a great deal of our understanding of past life regression and in reincarnation stem from this reservoir. It isn't that we lived in the past but we are directly connected to it.

The triad of hamr-hugr-hamingja represents the Verdandi portion. These are the tools for each fleeting moment of "that which is becoming". This is the constant transitioning between the objective, subjective, and noujective realms. They can be used to alter the self, evaluate options and even bring additional powers to bear on external activity. At times these can appear to be separate from the normal order and effects of causality.

The triad of Sal-Odr-Ond represents the Skuld portion. This complex is always under development into "that which ought become" whether done consciously or not. While the other triads represent a certain potential or a set of options the synergy of these three allows for the limitless and truly unique. These components are rarely tapped into but do show themselves at such times as getting into the "Zone", "Flow", and "Rapture" (peak performance, optimal experience, hyper emotion).

No Pain No Gain

The path less traveled is not an easy one. It should be understood that self-awakening and creation of a soul requires work. If you want to build a strong, shapely body you must exercise, this is a function of working against nature (gravity, resistance, etc.). If you want to improve mental functions you must exercise the mind. This cannot be a rote memorization of someone else's thoughts. It requires a digesting of information and experience to synthesize your own enlightenment usually by going against the commonly held beliefs. The spirit although remote to our understanding must be noujectively exercised as well through higher emotion. In many ways there is an overlap and interconnection between the body-mind-soul complex and exercising each benefits the others.

Exercising the physical comes in many forms but begins by keeping the body supplied with the proper nutrition, work and rest. The body's cells remember past actions through genetic memory that can be activated by reproducing activities your ancestors performed. The best balance would be training in new endeavors until they become mechanical and spending time performing (remembering) ancient tasks of some sort (blacksmithing, weaving, etc.). Then the hamr must be supplied with many different stimuli in order for it to experience and process them into useful energies. This would include the painful as well as the pleasurable and those in between on a sensory basis. It is best to avoid illegal actions since they could lead to a limitation on future options or intolerable levels that could blind you to the experience. Absorbing these experiences will strengthen the sal in order for it to be easier to identify and tap into in a controlled way. Harnessing it can generate phenomenal physical abilities and feelings.

In addition to memorization exercises designed to improve faculty performance, learning from your history is critical. Training the memory requires attention to activities as they happen in order to record a stronger impression making recall easier. Seeking out new experiences with this type of focus will give more information to be processed for storage and learning. Absorbing all this information is worthless without reflection. Turning your thoughts on these facts and arranging them into new patterns is the job of the mind. Experiment with ideas that may be taboo and change your point of view to see things from a new angle. Brainstorming of this type will sharpen this mental faculty to a razor's edge. But most of all it is best to Think, period. Do not accept anything at face value without first analyzing it for yourself. Realize how frequently you go through life blocking out your own thoughts and stop it. Slowly you will awaken the sleeping giant of inspiration releasing powers and insights never dreamed of: a creative level that will allow you to solve any mundane problem with a blink of an eye.

On to the realm of inner work, this is the hardest area of work because the spiritual world is mysterious and elusive. It is exactly that reason that makes it necessary. The reward is worth it as Don Webb explains "The simple act of doing what is hard merely to gain power over yourself creates a true Power. As it continues in your life, you will have less need of ritual, and will see more and more that things come about simply because you speak of them." (pg5). Here work will be conducted on the noujective world and deep seeded emotions. Learn to speak to your inner self and listen to your gut on this level. Many times our emotions are whispering in our ear but we are too distracted to hear. They have given us a thousand lifetimes to learn from if we will just ask. Quiet inward meditation is the best tool for getting these impressions in a tangible way and then harnessing them to your purposes. Using those impressions you can then send lady luck out to roll the dice in your favor. Each time dynamic emotion is successfully directed toward a goal it is strengthened in the process. A great deal of advancement in this arena can be made through the study and practice of magic indigenous to the Germanic people (runes, galdor, and seidhr) where these techniques and more are developed. When you have touched the divine in yourself and that flame ignites nothing in Midgard will be denied you.

Triad

It is the Sal-Odr-Ond triad that we may get our first glimpse of divine possibilities. Souls will differ in manifestation somewhat due to the nature of the body-mind-spirit development of each individual. It is this development we want to take charge of.

We can see from the self-complex a potential energy manifestation in the Sal-Odr-Ond triad. We have already discussed the tripartite nature of man and the nature of entropy. Here we have a solution for how they can be directed. When we say immortality, we are speaking of a permanent individual existence of the Self-identity through a Divinely Ascended Immortal Soul. Consciousness can cause effects across dimensions, that is part of what being Awake means. Normally portions of our self-complex remain subconscious and other parts beyond consciousness. We can see these occasionally as Carroll points out in *Liber Null & Psychonaut*,

> "There is almost nothing we can say of it [Kia, Spirit] except that it is the void center of consciousness, and it 'is' what it touches. It does not have any qualities like goodness, compassion, or spirituality, nor their opposites. It does, however, give a feeling of meaning or consciousness when we experience or will anything, and it becomes more apparent to us when we experience something powerfully. Laughter in ecstasy gives us a glimpse of it." (164)

The normal process for most people is to stay a fractured being and upon death of the body, consciousness dissolves into thought forms that merge with the Astral dimension, or it provides emotional energy to the Ethereal. Atoms from the body feed the Material dimension. The natural flow for energy as we have discussed is to manifest in the sal-odr-ond. The nature of the left-hand path is to bind that energy to the Self. Through the Dark Arts of Immortality we will grow the sal-odr-ond by our actions, words, and will and then bind that energy to become a Divinely Ascended Immortal Soul. With the binding of this energy to the Self-identity and the timelessness of our altered consciousness and being we can think of our physical death as the birth of a god.

VII. Hidden Powers

*The human being is a relation, a "synthesis," namely,
a synthesis of finitude and infinity, of possibility and necessity,
of the temporal and the eternal.*
-Gunter Figal

We are told that we use less than 10% of our brain capacity. In reality we also use only about 10% of our potential in other areas. Look at the activities of the average person and you will agree with me. Time in daily life is wasted, therefore wasted potential. Most people don't try to improve or learn everyday, wasted potential. Most people don't think for themselves, they allow advertisers to do it for them, wasted potential. Most people don't exercise their body to anywhere near full capability, not even to its mean, wasted potential. You are already in the elite percentage of people simply by the fact that you are thinking enough for yourself to investigate this work. Hopefully you are elitist in the other areas I just mentioned.

There are states of consciousness (peak performance, optimal experience, hyper emotion) reached in rare instances by most people. Some states of being result in an elevation of physical prowess, some in a sensual pleasure, and some an expansion of awareness (i.e. fury, ecstasy, exaltation). These are a glimpse at what is possible. Generally they are uncontrollable because the mechanism that causes them is unknown to the person at the time and they are fleeting, which makes them difficult to comprehend. Also their contradictory elements make it confusing to study and recreate. But what if we could harness the benefits of higher consciousness when desired and utilize these states of being to power our actions, words, and will to extreme levels. Our impact on the Universe and our Selves would be miraculous.

At some point in everyone's life they ask the question, "Why am I here?" Maybe someone somewhere has the perfect answer to it but I've never heard it. Maybe the problem getting a good answer is because we ask the wrong question. The question should be, "Since I am here what should I be doing?"

The answer to this question comes in many forms, but it is possible to come up with some really good ones and a few great ones. Part of the answer is finding out who you are by nature. What examples of great lives can we find? What plan did the Gods/esses have in mind when they created us? Or, if we are evolving, how are we doing; and to what end will we arrive? We have already investigated the myths briefly. If they are communications from the God/esses or simply ancient wisdom we have some answers. Within Germanic culture, our ancestors have basically left instructions through their traditions and oral teachings in the forms of heroic literature and runic keys. Here we will take a look at some of the traditional beliefs and how they fit within the concepts we have covered so far. It is apparent the techniques we will be discussing have been in use for thousands of years, albeit unwittingly. To help discover our true self, we will go back in time to before the schism in our nature (warrior/lover/magician) or at the minimum to a time when we recognized the problem. The myths tell us what our ancestors believed about the nature of Man.

Immortality and Spiritual Eugenics

The most important words regarding the Germanic beliefs in immortality come from the *Poetic Edda*, specifically from the *Havamal* (sayings of the high one) stanzas 76 & 77.

> *Cattle die, kinsmen die,*
> *thyself too soon will die;*
> *but renown will never fade,*
> *I envy him who wins it.*

> *Cattle die, kinsmen die,*
> *thyself too soon will die;*
> *one thing I know will never wither:*
> *the obligation upon each one dead.*

This is a rough translation of the original poem. The meaning passed on by this poetry requires knowledge of the ancient culture. The words used in stanza one (76) are translated by various authors and parallel meaning very well. The second stanza has been translated exactly like the first by many authors, but they miss the point of meaning in the word *doomr*. The word was used alternatively for judgment, obligation, and opinion. The last part of that line means 'in contact with the individual' but implies still somehow part of a whole. Since the first stanza is fairly clear and points to the immortality of the individual left here in the physical world through their fame or glory the second one must be referring to the afterlife. This is certainly the case when we look at 'obligation in contact with the dead'. If they don't continue to exist then nothing can be 'in contact'. The implication makes sense; they have an obligation to the living and to their self that continues into the afterlife. This could be a direct reference to the hero's obligation to save humanity by becoming an Einherjar or Valkyrie.

When examining the Germanic beliefs about immortality we come away with two main themes: the idea of renown (stanza 76) and personal ascension (stanza 77). From the description of Valhalla and Folkvangr we can see it is not a place where souls go to rest and wait for rebirth. It is a place where the ascended train and grow in a dynamic environment in preparation for battle (strife). According to Rudolf Simek in *The Dictionary of Northern Mythology* he defines soul and in it he says the Germanic peoples did not have a concept of a preexisting soul. They definitely believed in spirit. The only way both of these can be reconciled is by the idea that the soul is manifested (created) through life experiences. We have seen how the sal-odr-ond triad within the Germanic self-complex and time context expressed that concept.

Eugenics is the science that deals with the improvement of the hereditary qualities of a race or breed. It is basically the practice of selective breeding in order to propagate the best genetic traits. The idea is to slowly improve the species (plant, animal, etc.) over successive generations. The "best genetic traits" is debatable. Some people may like peaches without fur (called nectarines) but others may not consider it an improvement. In fact some would suggest the flavor is not the same, a small change in flavor is the sacrifice you make to grow one without fur. None-the-less we can apply the practice to spirit in the same manner. It is possible to pass on certain traits and improve them over successive generations. Remember the blueprint for spirit is just potential it can be developed and changed throughout life experiences. Dr. Stephen Flowers, in *Studia Germanica Vol. 1*, speaks of something that could be the spiritual blueprint and potential and are explained this way,

> "*Aptrburdhr* and the institutional rites of passage seem to converge in the Norse conceptions of psychophysical and cultic realities to describe a process in which ancestral forces contained in definite entities are passed from generation to generation, and maintained and developed by ritual formulas and ethical behavior... These [fylgja, hamingja] appear to be the primary entities that are 'reborn' through the generations." (32)

The obvious way to pass on spiritual traits is related to breeding practices designed to unite individuals with similar supra-conscious development. This will increase the likely hood of supra-consciousness developing in progeny.

Naming rites practiced by the ancient Germans did something similar. Since growth and development are influenced by potential and experience they would name a child after an ancestor. The child would be brought up on tales of the relative's deeds. By mimicking the ancestor's adventures they would develop similar qualities. Some believed the ancestor's spirit would literally be reborn. Either way this method encompasses two possibilities, one by using genetic characteristics (potential through bloodline) and the second utilizes a duplication of experience. So by naming offspring after ancestors who achieved high levels of Being we can multiply the odds of the genetic predisposition. Rick Fields explains why renown was so important to the warrior,

> "Yet the heroic warrior was no mere materialist, no merchant or trader. Success in battle - prowess - not wealth, was the final measure of the warrior. Greater even than honor counted in plunder was the public recognition the warrior won when the bards sang of his great deeds - his *aristeia*. When that happened the warrior's honor was transformed and extended into the future as *kleos*, fame and glory sung by the wandering court bards to future generations of warriors. This glory justified and fulfilled his existence, since it demonstrated that he had proven himself worthy of his ancestors, that he continued his heroic lineage and bequeathed it to his descendants." (70)

Renown is another way of performing spiritual eugenics that is similar to naming but extends outside of familial lines. By modeling your life or that of a child (could include naming) you produce an increased possibility for supra-consciousness and spiritual advancement. It also helps humanity by spreading these traits way beyond the bounds of physical reproduction. Dr. Flowers also has this to say in *Studia Germanica Vol. 1*,

> "**Aptrburdhr* may be strictly said to be the transference of powers, abilities, characteristics, "fate," etc. (but not necessarily of the 'personality') of a dead ancestor to an unborn descendant... Subsequent "rites of passage" test and demonstrate the validity of this transference." (31)

Renown is also a method of achieving a form of immortality.

Ragnarok

Ragnarok translated literally means something like Twilight of the Gods or Doom of the Gods. Although it undergoes some major transformation during the Viking era, its roots in Germanic culture grow out of the very dim past. The Ragnarok is a war between the Thurses (giants) and the Gods/esses. In the myth there will be a titanic battle when the Fire giants come and attempt to exterminate mankind. The Gods/esses intervene along with an army of ascended humans called Valkyrie (females) and Einherjar (males).

Why would the Gods/esses risk destruction to protect humanity? The question also arises why did the Gods/esses create us in the first place? Are we purely for entertainment? Food? Pets? Of course everyone would like to think we serve some higher purpose. It is probable we bring something to the Universe the Gods/esses don't have. Whatever the reason, the fact is we are here. Since we are here, what should we do about it? In the myth of Ragnarok, the ascended humans fight alongside the Gods/esses to prevent this genocide. If we eliminate the thought of creation and look at this as just another myth our ancestors used to pass on knowledge, does it change in importance? I don't think so. The aspiration to become ascended beings of that capability still sounds noble to me.

The argument also comes up that the Gods/esses should increase their numbers. Why wouldn't they just create more Gods/esses to handle the situation? Odin procreated Thor the greatest divine warrior. He alone has destroyed numerous giants. Odin procreated Vali, the divine avenger, and is also credited with many other divine birthings (definitely a master of the art of sex). Why would he need man (albeit semi-divine ascended ones) in the battle when he can create Gods? The only possible answer is because man must bring something to the table the Gods/esses cannot provide for themselves. This bears itself out in the heroic traditions and runic hints. We indeed have power.

Valhalla and Folkvangr

So where do all these ascended humans come from? Why, from a warrior's paradise of course. Actually there are two of them in Norse mythology. Everyone has probably heard of Valhalla. But there is a second hall named Folkvangr that mirrors it. They are described as vast structures built of gold and silver with five hundred doors. At the time of the Ragnarok eight hundred warriors will dash from each door into battle. To the Norse a hundred actually meant one hundred and twenty so if you do the math, doors times warriors times two halls you end up with a figure of a little under 1.3 million ascended humans.

Valhalla is in Asgard in the abode of Odin. The warriors there fight all day training for this confrontation with the fire giants. At dawn all the dead (metaphorically speaking, since they are already dead) arise. They feast and drink all night only to start the cycle over again the next morning. The new existence of these ascended humans is described by Dr. Flowers in *Black Runa*,

> "Existence in Walhalla is of a threefold character: (1) It is above all *active*, constant endeavor of one kind or another. (2) It is *pleasurable*, usually being described as feasting and entertainment in the hall. (3) It has *great purpose* as preparation for the "final conflict" in which the world will be transformed and renewed." (26)

Due in part to the misogynistic nature of the monotheistic religions that swept through Europe, the hall of Folkvangr is not as well known as Valhalla. It is basically a mirror image of Valhalla but is in the abode of Freya in the world of Vanaheim. It says in *Gylfaginning* that Freya gets half of the slain heroes and in fact she chooses first. Obviously her hall is equally manned (or wo-manned), and it would not be a stretch to suggest that the daily battles and training takes place between combatants from both paradises. Another feminine aspect that was lost was the nature of the female warriors and their respective numbers. The Valkyrie are at times relegated to serving maids and number only in the dozens. There are many reasons for this, especially the incursion of other religions and the monopolization of the written word. With a little work it becomes clear the Valkyrie and Einherjar are both cut from the same mold and surely have equal representation.

This suppression of women and of the Goddesses during the Middle Ages led also to a conspicuous absence of them from the Ragnarok myth. It would be silly to disregard them considering the many surviving tales of women warriors, and the fact that one of Freya's major spheres of influence was war and the leadership of the Valkyrie. Since the description of the Ragnarok shows only one location of the battle, it could be that the forces led by Freya are attacking the home of the Fire giants. Attacking an enemy's less defended territory while they are away battling elsewhere has always been a good strategy.

The point to be made by all this is that there was a strong belief among the ancient Germans in divine ascension. That heavenly existence was active and dynamic. That man's life here was important and his actions affected the future of all mankind, and that once ascended he or she could stand toe to toe with other Divine Beings. Dr. Flowers, in *Black Runa*, adds,

> "In the teaching of Walhalla we recognize the Essence of the Left Hand Path. The heroes who dwell there are immortal and unique, individual participants in a process of evolution of which both they and the cosmos partake. They are *active* agents in this process of Becoming." (26)

An examination of the mythology of the Valkyrie and Einherjar will enlighten us as to a path toward ascension. Our ancestors had a clear idea of what was required to become a Divinely Ascended Immortal Soul in the service of a greater purpose for all humankind.

Valkyrie and Einherjar

As I said the ascended humans are called Valkyrie and Einherjar. Valkyrie means 'choosers of the slain', and Einherjar means something like 'single champion'. Over time the connection between the two has become somewhat disjointed. Yes, they still interact in the myths and heroic literature but the rolls have changed and merged. Some of the confusion occurs because of different authors during different time periods emphasizing certain aspects to the exclusion of others, or cultural and religious pressures caused some elements to be altered or left out entirely. This alteration caused an obscuring of the origin of the ascended humans. Now we ask the questions: where do the ascended humans come from and how do they do it? The pieces of the puzzle come together to clarify the origins of the stories and legends. There were ancient cults of Odin and Freya and those followers exhibited extraordinary powers leading to the differing fairy tales and supernatural legends. One cult led to the most recent tales of the Wild Hunt and the other held over in the stories of Valpurgisnacht (Witch's Night). Both of these legendary cultic groups originated from one central Germanic tribe in history, the Harii.

Since they have undergone the most dramatic change we will start with the Valkyrie, which I have explained means choosers of the slain. Modern versions of the Valkyrie stir up images of chain mail clad vixens with winged helmets and spears riding through the clouds to aid their chosen champions in battle. In some legends they appeared to heroes in troubled times to pass on learning or to protect them. Then they would guide these dead heroic souls to Valhalla (part of the reason for the term choosers of the slain). Davidson shows the reason for the link with magic and spirit by saying,

> "We recognize [in Valkyries] something akin to the Norns, spirits who decide the destinies of men; to the seeresses, who could protect men in battle by their spells; to the powerful female guardian spirits attached to certain families, bringing luck to a youth under their protection; even to certain women who armed themselves and fought like men, ...also of the priestesses of war, women who officiated at the sacrificial rites..." (61)

She also confirms the ascension aspects of the Valkyrie with "Human princesses are said to become Valkyries, as though they were the priestesses of some cult." (61). Here we see signs in a belief that a human woman could achieve divine like status. It also points to the over-woman nature of the individual with 'human princesses.'

In the oldest stories, though, the Valkyries were dark terrifying female warriors who rode through the sky to rain down death and carnage on the battlefields. Older still are stories of ghastly wolf-women. The transition took centuries and found its way through many forms as H. R. Ellis-Davidson confirms:

> "There is little doubt that the figure of the Valkyrie has developed in Norse literature into something more dignified and less blood-thirsty as a result of the work of the poets over a considerable period. The alarming and terrible creatures who have survived in the literature in spite of this seem likely however to be closer in character to the choosers of the slain as they were visualized in heathen times." (66)

The Old English cognate to Valkyrie is *waelcyrge*. It is more akin to werewolves than to pretty amazons with winged helmets. The stories left over about these, *waelcyrge* stem from dark phantom like women pouring blood over the battlefield or picking through the dead remains. Davidson describes them as near monsters "Female creatures, ...carrying troughs of blood or riding on wolves." (61). This 'riding on wolves' or possibly being dressed as wolves is reflected in the Sabbat orgies of Witch's Night. *Waelcyrge* was often used to gloss over the word witch and Davidson sites the most well known occasion "...an Anglo-Saxon bishop, Wulfstan, included 'choosers of the slain' [*Waelcyrge*] in a black list of sinners, witches, and evil-doers in his famous *Sermo Lupi* [Sermon of the Wolf]. All the other classes whom he mentions are human ones, and it seems unlikely that he has introduced mythological figures as well." (61). This would certainly point to the fact that the legends of these werewolf type women had some basis in actuality rather than urban myth. So where would we find dark sorceress/warrior women possibly dressed as wolves creating a fiendish appearance on the battlefield?

All through the transformation of the Valkyrie the Einherjar maintain a close connection to their roots. It was only the cultic appearance that seemed to change. The Einherjar remained a warrior type being where as the Valkyrie went from demonic predator to pristine spirit guide. H. M. Chadwick is not convinced of this strictly spiritual aspect when he says in *The Cult of Othin*,

> "But it is at least questionable if in actual religious belief they occupied the same position, which is ascribed to them in the poetry. They [Valkyrie] are elsewhere (Volsunga s. 2 etc.) called Othin's *oskmeyiar* "adopted maidens" (or "daughters"). With this may be compared the expression *oskasynir*, "adopted sons," in Gylf. 20: "all those who fall in battle are called Othins' *oskasynir*. The more usual term for the latter is however *einherjar*, which signifies perhaps merely "champions." (10)

Here we find the Valkyrie and Einherjar placed into distinctly equal classification. Much of their true nature is still hidden though.

We already mentioned the hidden nature of the cults of Odin and Freya in a previous section. Georges Dumezil sheds some light on the age of these secret groups in *Destiny of the Warrior* saying,

> "Odhinn's elect surely form a "band," a men's society, such as abounded among the Vikings; but the type was as old as the Germanic world. Proof is furnished by the very name of Odinn's elect, the Einherjar (**aina-harija-*), the second element of which is not other than the name of an ancient people of continental Germany, the Harii, whom Tacitus (*Germania*, re.t) quite appropriately depicts as such a men's society, although without entirely understanding its mechanism." (112)

When Tacitus speaks of the Harii he is not speaking of a cult per se, but a tribe of people. In his own words:

> "I need only give the names of the most powerful: the Harii,... As for the Harii, not only are they superior in strength to the other peoples I have just mentioned, but they minister to their savage instincts by trickery and clever timing. They black their shields and dye their bodies, and choose pitch dark nights for their battles. The shadowy, awe-inspiring appearance of such a ghoulish army inspires mortal panic; for no enemy can endure a sight so strange and hellish. Defeat in battle starts always with the eyes." (137, translation by H. Mattingly, revised translation S. A. Hanford)

This description predates the Ninja, Assassins, and Thugee by a thousand years. It is interesting to note the left hand path nature of all three of these organizations (the turning point for the assassins coming about 1164 C. E., coincidentally the same time as their interaction with the Knights Templar). Also interesting is the origin of Ninjitsu from west of China from a line called the Hatori and the name of the leader of the Assassins (Old Man of the Mountain) is similar to *Ala-Odin*.

This description of the Harii is very familiar from our discussion of the Wild Hunt with their black painted riders and wolves. They ride through the sky chanting runes to paralyze those without sense enough to hide. In the area around the tribal territory of the Harii have come inscriptions to a God Harigast and Goddess Hariasa. Odin and Freya both had multiple names in fact Odin's number in excess of a hundred and fifty. De Vries has identified Harigast as referring to Odin. Hariasa has been identified as a Goddess of war and is related to valkyrie names of battle. Surely this Goddess is Freya.

If a warrior is strong enough in battle and heroic enough in his life upon his death he will be raised to the ghostly world of Valhalla or Folkvangr. There he takes on the title Einherjar. The term is often used though to describe individual humans on the path to becoming a semi-divine Being. Throughout the literature the Einherjar are also connected with the animal pelt wearing berserkers. Rick Fields sees this as a way to change the mindset of the warrior, "The fully initiated warrior was thus also the fully metamorphosed warrior. He had entered an altered or extraordinary state of consciousness which freed him from the inhibitions (or fear or reluctance) against killing another human being." (63). One of these cultic bands (*mannerbund*) of berserkers wore wolf pelts and called *Ulfhedhnar*. The main purpose of this use of black paint and wolf pelt wearing was twofold. The first being the transformation brought about in the wearer of such coverings. It was a sign the person had changed into something other than human. This not only gave them courage and strength, but it also put them outside of the rules of man. He or she was no longer a part of that society. The second, and more obvious, benefit is the one Tacitus mentions. The sheer terror it could produce in the enemy. This attack on the will was the first step toward defeat for them. It became a very universal practice as Rick Fields says in *Code of the Warrior*, "The shadowy figures of the Indo-European *mannerbund*, the warrior bands, howling, painted, tattooed, wrapped in the pelts of bear and wolf, can be glimpsed in myths and tales from Ireland to India." (60).

The Harii was a Germanic tribe of antiquity first mentioned by Tacitus in 50 C. E. That tribe used a tactic of painting themselves and their equipment black and attacking in an un-characteristic manner at the time, at night. There is evidence of them wearing wolf skins to add to the hellish sight. It was not uncommon in the region for women to fight along side the men. Certainly if a tribe resorted to these guerilla tactics it was probably short on numbers and would make up for it in strength, magic, trickery, and the use of able bodied women. There is ample evidence of their cultic worship of Odin and Freya. It is also evident this cult had magical as well as martial prowess.

Considering the fact that wolves entered the battlefield to scavenge the dead it is not unlikely that a small tribe (cult) that used scare tactics would want to recover their wounded and continue their phantom impression by leaving no trace. The concept of 'choosers of the slain' and hence *Wealcyrge* (Valkyrie) could easily have come from the wolf-pelt clad women not only fighting with the men but recovering the dead after the battle through the disguise of scavenger. This tribe kept up its ghostly appearance by keeping its cult underground for millennia. All of this points to the cults of Odin and Freya that moved through Europe as the Wild Hunt and Valpurgisnacht myths had their origin in the tribe of the Harii. The nature of these cults was divine ascension: creation of Valkyrie and Einherjar.

Heroic Legends

I could not imagine a better way to open this section than with the words of Dr. Stephen E. Flowers from *Studia Germanica*, "The study of heroic models of human, or praeter-human, behavior is essential to the understanding of a traditional people because such myths provide a bridge between the archetypal realm of gods and goddesses and ordinary human beings." (ix).

There are many examples of heroic stories in the literature and folklore of the Germanic peoples. They all reflect similar uses of the Dark Arts (war, sex, magic). There are two figures that stand out among all of those. Their renown is unparalleled in Germanic literature and that is reason enough to speak of them. Ironically enough they both share the pages of the same book. As stories go they are the near archetypal Valkyrie and Einherjar. I am speaking of course of Brynhild and Sigurd from *Saga of the Volsungs*. They have been immortalized in *Richard Wagner's* opera *The Ring Cycle* and another German epic called the *Nibelungilied*. There have also been histories and novels written about them. I will not attempt to challenge those efforts. All I wish to do here is illuminate the use of the Dark Arts within the volumes of literature about them. It signifies a belief held very strongly by the Germanic people and it helps guide us along the path. The Saga of the Volsungs details the life of the Volsung family from the adventures of Sigi (Sigurd's great-great-grand father) beyond the death of Sigurd and Brynhild. Many scholars have focused on Sigurd in their studies. I, however, will show the importance of the life of Brynhild as well. It is a prime feminine example of the Dark Arts (personal combat, sexual fantasy, mystic rituals) in use and the rebelling against the societal order (fecundity, force, sovereignty).

The part involving Sigurd starts with his childhood. He is born after the death of his father and is raised by Regin. A foster father raises Brynhild as well. Sigurd is educated in the secrets of the forge (presumably weapon-smithing since that was Regin's avocation), various languages, mental games and physical contests. When Sigurd is grown Regin attempts twice to forge a sword with which Sigurd can kill a dragon for its treasure. The dragon is well known to Regin, being a transformed family member. He fails on the first two attempts. Sigurd retrieves the fragments of his father's shattered sword and provides these to Regin for a third attempt at creating a weapon that will penetrate the dragon's scales. They succeed in re-forging Gram (the sword).

Sigurd's first transgression occurs against the warrior function. He kills the dragon not by facing it in the manner of a true warrior but by using trickery. After the death of the dragon Sigurd unwittingly performs an act of magic. He cooks the heart of Fafnir (the dragon) and after burning his finger (pain) he tastes of it and his mind is expanded. Then he commits what could be classified as his sin against sovereignty or against fecundity, he kills Regin (who was planning betrayal). Regin could fit either category since he is a producer (craftsman and wealth because he was entitled to half the dragons treasure) and priest-king (because he was Sigurd's mentor and tutor).

It is here that Brynhild enters the story. Odin has stabbed her with a sleep thorn. Her first transgression is a double sin against sovereignty. She disobeys Odin, a God, and she kills a king (the one Odin wished to be victorious in battle). Behind a wall of shields she lies still dressed in full armor. Sigurd manages to awaken her. They have both heard of the others great reputation. As a reward for helping her, Brynhild counsels Sigurd in wisdom and magical charms (runes). His words win her over and her beauty wins him. Both were skilled in the art of sex and seduction and these are the only times in the tale they are happy. They pledge vows to each other and go their separate ways both to gain more glory in battle. The dark art of war is evident from the descriptions of both warriors who seem supernaturally skilled in personal combat. They meet again at Brynhild's foster family's kingdom where Sigurd commits another 'sin' by deceiving the king. Brynhild continues her art of sex by appealing to Sigurd's ego. Brynhild is a master of prophecy and often warns people of future events to no avail. They separate again and Brynhild gives birth to their child.

Sigurd arrives in another kingdom and is given a magic drink to make him forget Brynhild so the queen's stepdaughter (Gudrun) can marry him. Sigurd rides off with her brother (Gunnar) to help him acquire a woman of his own. Gunnar is unsuccessful so Sigurd shape changes (art of magic) into Gunnar's likeness and here Sigurd 'sins' against fecundity by deceiving a woman into marrying who she thinks is Gunnar. This woman is none other than Brynhild whom Sigurd does not recognize because of the potion of forgetfulness and she does not recognize him of course because he is shape changed. It is not important that he violates his oath to Brynhild by marrying Gudrun because he is bewitched. But Brynhild transgresses against fecundity by agreeing to marry the man who passed through a wall of flames after already committing herself to Sigurd earlier.

So now Brynhild comes to live with Gunnar whom she thinks won her. In the same kingdom resides her in-laws Gudrun and of course her husband Sigurd whom Brynhild recognizes. The plot thickens as the forgetfulness spell on Sigurd wears off and Brynhild discovers the truth about the shape changing trickery. Brynhild decides to stir up trouble (sin against sovereignty) for the princess Gudrun. In her scheming Brynhild commits her sin against force (warrior function). She convinces others to kill Sigurd instead of facing him herself. She then places herself on his funeral pyre and ascends with him.

I have only described a small fraction of the Saga. It would be useful for you to read it along with other heroic stories. The tragic nature of the poem should not detract from its wonder and power. That was the most popular genre in that time period. What should stand out is the fame both characters have won for themselves. It is obvious they were both masters of the Dark Arts of war, sex, and magic. The success of their deeds within the body of the work is telling of the type of personal power they both achieved by synthesizing the Dark Arts. The transgressions or 'sins' against the societal divisions should also not detract from the integrity of the characters. They are there to reinforce the antinomian nature necessary for true growth. To this day, the word Valkyrie brings to mind Brynhild and Sigurd is the first man thought of when the word Einherjar is mentioned.

Runic Hints

The word 'rune' actually means secret or mystery. It has come to be used for the symbol system and magical alphabet called the runes. But in reality they are much more than either. The runes are an esoteric mystery tradition. Odin won the knowledge of the runes after a magical ordeal. After being wounded by a spear he hung himself on the world tree (axis of the world) for nine days without food or drink. This is a textbook use of magic and an archetypal one as well. The significance of the world tree is that the axis means it is the center from which all cause and effect emanates therefore placing himself at the origin of (hence unaffected by) the temporal. He took them wailing, which shows he was in pain and not shut off from himself (bridging the worlds). He passed that knowledge to man in the form of a symbol system called the runes. A group of rune masters codified this knowledge in various ways to include several rune poems. The extent of that knowledge goes way beyond the scope of this work. I will however include a couple examples.

Each individual rune (letter) had a full name and that name was a word with meaning. From the cultural understanding of the word and by deciphering the clues left by the runemasters of old we can gain great insight into the knowledge they passed on. One of the major branches of esoteric knowledge about the runes was left in the form of rune poems. Edred Thorsson explains it this way in *Runelore*, "The original purpose of these works may have been to help the runemasters hold certain key concepts in mind while performing runecastings, or they may have just been traditional formulations of the general lore of the runes." (93). You could think of them as mental puzzles or like zen koans. At first reading the lines don't seem related or to make sense but just like an oxymoron (i.e. bittersweet) once experienced they are an epiphany. They help strengthen the mind and the will. There are at least four rune poems and by comparing the descriptions among them an even deeper understanding will come.

For my example I have chosen the three runes for the word ART (Ansuz, Raidho, and Tiwaz) from just the Old Norwegian Rune Rhyme. Their symbols look like this - ᚠᚱᛏ. When drawn together into a common theme or working they are called bind-runes. I have named this one the Rune-sword since all three (and they are the only ones) have elements of sword making or use. It is instructive that swords were given names in heroic stories because they were thought of as persons. It was also believed they could be connected to spirits of ancestors. The hamingja or fylja (spiritual components of the Germanic self-complex) could be attached to a weapon and physically passed down the family line. All of this leads to the idea of a sword as a metaphor for Man. The names of three runes and their poem verses follow.

Ansuz-Raidho-Tiwaz

[Estuary] is the way of most journeys;
but the sheath is [that for] swords.

[Riding], it is said, is the worst for horses;
Reginn forged the best sword.

[Tyr] is the one-handed among the Aesir;
the smith has to blow often.

In the Old Norwegian Rune Rhyme these three mention the sword or the process of making a sword. When deciphered and combined with the knowledge gleaned from the Old English Rune Poem and the Old Icelandic Rune Poem they deliver a compelling description of the path for ascension. It is wisdom we are attempting to gain and wisdom they were trying to transmit. It only requires a little cultural background knowledge to begin to unwrap the enigma of the runes.

In a nutshell, this bind-rune represents the idea of the individual choosing the difficult 'road less traveled' in true antinomian fashion. This is a direct acknowledgement of the principles of the Left Hand Path. Odin and Freya set this example and even Sigurd and Brynhild for a time refused to stay together in order to advance their own personal growth. We would do well to follow their example. This is not a one-time thing to be done on occasion it is an all the time thing.

The Ansuz stanzas compare an estuary and sheath. These two lines seem totally unrelated upon first reading. But it is very easy to understand when in the light of a little ancient culture. An estuary is an inlet from the sea, a safe harbor if you will. That is exactly how our ancestors viewed it: a nice comfortable place to park your ship. The comparison is made to a sheath because it is the same thing symbolically for a sword. A sword is in the scabbard only when things are quiet and safe. As I said already, a sword is a metaphor for a man. The line 'is the way of most journeys' means that most people take the safe way, the estuary. It is countered by the admonishment of similarity to a sheath. A sword is not meant to be in the scabbard and to the ancient Germans a ship was not to be in the estuary. Both are meant to be used in war and to face risk in the pursuit of life and achievement. The sword is meant to be drawn in battle, and likewise we are not to seek shelter in the estuary but to brave the dangers of the open ocean in the pursuit of experience. We are to choose the more difficult road.

Raidho represents the process of the quest. To the ancients the horse represented mobility, travel, and adventure. The comparison to the horse revolves around the concept that the horse is ridden and led along the path. It does not choose it's own way necessarily and that is why it is worse for it. It is countered by the next section pointing out we need to choose our own path not be led along. We touched briefly on the story involving Regin the smith in

Saga of the Volsungs. Normally a person would read these stanzas and have no concept of whom he was. After Regin fails to make the sword the second time Sigurd brings him the raw materials. Depending on which version you read he either succeeds the third time or Sigurd forges it with what he learned from Regin. The point of this comparison is again related to the sword and man symbolism. The sword, the stanza says is the 'best' is Sigurd himself not his sword, Gram. Regin raised Sigurd and taught him to think for himself. He showed him how to forge for himself. Sigurd provided the raw material and then far surpassed Regin in ability and renown on his own with what he had learned. We learn from the mythology of Odin and Freya and all the heroic legends the concept of the quest but we must walk the path for ourselves.

Tiwaz is used to enforce the idea of continued work. Again without a basic background in Norse mythology a person reading this stanza would be lost. Tyr is a God who sacrificed his hand to save the other Gods/esses. In the myth he has to place his hand in the mouth of a great wolf as a pledge that the Gods/esses were not trying to trick it. Tyr knew they were trying to trick the beast and that they must succeed in binding him or everyone would suffer. So he knew going in he would lose the hand to its anger of realization. They succeed in trapping the wolf and forever after Tyr is associated with this single act of bravery and sacrifice. The next stanza counters this with the idea it is not a single action that you should strive to be remembered for but repeated action that brings greatness. It is only through repeated action that one even has a chance to attempt and succeed at something great. A smith does not blow on the fire once, heat the metal once, hammer it once, and temper it once. It takes a thousand times repeating this process to create a supreme weapon. When we remember that the weapon is a man, we realize immediately the truth of this stanza. A single act of sacrifice nor a single act of bravery does not define a Man. The true hero lives with these everyday of his life.

That completes the Rune-sword bindrune. In order to reach ascension we must choose for ourselves the difficult path and follow it all the time. This represents only a fraction of the wisdom available within the mysteries (runes). We have only scratched the surface here and have not even touched on the magical (self-transformational) uses. It is sad to think how much of this knowledge is not being taken advantage of in our modern society. Only one thing I can think of is worse, and that is to awaken to their wisdom and then fall back asleep. Reading the runes is a life's work in its own right. There are several periods of runic script and the number of symbols ranges from sixteen to thirty three. The number of possible combinations is almost limitless.

Before you fall back asleep it is time to choose your own path. The following chapters will elaborate on the Dark Arts of Immortality. The art of war (personal combat) is designed to teach you to reach the altered state of being called fury. The art of sex (sexual fantasy) is designed to teach you to reach the altered state of being called ecstasy. The art of magic (mystic ritual) is designed to teach you to reach the altered state of being called exaltation. Combined with antinomian practices and a change in the cycle of interaction with the Universe, it will be possible to synthesize their abilities. This cultic process worked well for our ancestors like the Harii and it will work even better for us. This is the secret to our hidden powers. Not only will you succeed in becoming an empowered individual in your lifetime, you will also be prepared to transform into a Divinely Ascended Immortal Soul.

VIII. Art of War

*Germans have no taste for peace;
renown is more easily won among perils,...*
                    -Cornelius Tacitus

The first dark art to be evaluated is war. The title for this chapter may be a bit misleading. In this chapter we are not going to delve into the details of mass battles or thermonuclear warfare. Nor even long term strategy. We are going to look at the fierce nature of human beings when engaged in the practice of warfare. We have already touched on some themes (memes, esses) in other chapters related to war. They had more to do with the broad macrocosmic picture which is a reflection of general human nature. We are going to look into the altered state of being and consciousness (fury) that is a direct result of the drives and tensions involved in Man that come out in war and empower the individual combatant. It is most likely to occur during real combat so war is where we most often recognize fury's presence. For our purposes though we need to find some other source for the attainment of fury in order to synthesize its benefits without the drawbacks.

You can see this same tendency toward microcosmic work in the ancient Germanic *mannerbund* (men's bands). These were the elite mercenary forces that formed the cults and secret societies of Odin and Freya. A large part of their occult practices was the direct harnessing of fury. As Dudley Young says "...war is not finally a political or a technological or even a psychological problem, but a religious one: we make war because the war gods call us to the field." (365). In the process we want to avoid the problem of the esse (or memes) of war controlling us. Barbara Ehrenreich sees the dilemma:

> "If war itself is thought of as something other than human - an abstract system that is "alive" in some formal, mathematical sense and preys on human societies - then warrior elites are the human form it takes. Through much of history it is they, and not the mass of ordinary people, who have made war, sought war, and celebrated war as a heroic, and even religious, undertaking." (150)

The reason this is the case is because the warrior elites gain something in the process while the rest of humanity does not. The esse of war controls the masses but the warrior elites tap personal power in war. We have to know exactly why we are doing this and the nature within ourselves that require its expression. Hopefully we can avoid the simplicity of Young's view when he says, "To have a war you need not covet your neighbor's ass nor even his goods: his wife and above all his territory will suffice." (71). The warrior elites know that ultimately the material possessions gained through war are immaterial. It is the growth of the warrior's Self that counts but the material possessions can help with attaining the necessary motivation for non-lethal combat as we shall see later.

This growth occurs from the confidence we gain from victory. The more we conquer our enemies the more we command ourselves. We are on the path to do both. Not only do we wish to raise our combative ability, but we also want to find the fastest way to achieve fury. One of the benefits of the death drive (Mortido) is the amount of energy that can be focused into physical action. There are sacrifices in mental and sensory function in order to produce this enhancement (see figure 7). We will use the word fury for the state of being we are interested in achieving in this art. Later we will develop it and mesh it with other states of being. For now stay focused on fury alone for as William James says, "The metaphysical mystery, thus recognized by common sense, that he who feeds on death that feeds on men [mortido] possesses life super eminently and excellently, and meets best the secret demands of the universe." (306). The key elements needed to reach the state of fury are anger, anxiety over the outcome of the conflict, and a powerful antagonist.

Fury

The aim of the art of war is to reach a supra-conscious state of being (fury). Fury is defined as an intense and destructive rage. It is further delineated as a state of being exhibiting extreme fierceness and violence. Dudley Young speaks of its chaotic tendencies by saying, "...and violence for the unarmed means rage, and rage is *par excellence* the emotion that moves into the unknown, the uncontrollable; and so when the moment comes it lacks decorum, and in fact if often looks like bloody mayhem." (70). This type of release, while not attractive per se, is the reason we are studying it in the first place. Civilized man has repressed some of his impulses to the point of numbness and mediocrity and misdirected the rest.

The word fury is related to the avenging spirits in mythology that inflicted the punishment of deities. At some point everyone has experienced the mind altering and body energizing effects of unbridled rage. James sees it as a part of man's nature to be violent and war as its perfect tool,

> "The beauty of war in this respect is that it is so congruous with ordinary human nature. Ancestral evolution has made us all potential warriors; so the most insignificant individual, when thrown into an army in the field, is weaned from whatever excess of tenderness toward his precious person he may bring with him, and may easily develop into a monster of insensibility." (308)

He is so right, but it (and we) could also be the tool of war itself. We have discussed the death drive (Mortido) already and the predilection to war comes from it. We want to harness this power for our own ends and we will find a way in non-lethal competition.

The ability to achieve this state is compounded by tension in the other drives as well. It will be helpful to take a look at the diagram (figure 7). It shows the major elements of fury entwined with ecstasy and exaltation. For our purposes it is a state of being which elevates the physical attributes of a person to preternatural levels. Strength, stamina and agility increase to inhuman capacity. Here we are reminded of the myths and legends of heroes stronger than ten men (i.e. Beowulf tearing off Grendel's arm). Accompanying this increase in physical abilities comes a corresponding decrease in sensory acuity (including pain sensitivity), and intense narrowing of awareness. This reduction of sensory sensation it shares with exaltation (art of magic), and the tunnel vision it shares with ecstasy (art of sex). Both inhibitors will have to be overcome later, but for now the main purpose is to experience fury frequently enough to become familiar with it within your self. The resulting supra-consciousness warps the perception of time.

The question is how do we achieve this excitement in our lives today. Some of the cultic methods used in the past are familiar to authors like Georges Dumezil as he shows with the following:

> "Their furor exteriorized a second being which lived with in them. The artifices of costume (cf. the *tincta copora* of the Harii), the disguises to which the name *berserkir* and its parallel *ulfhednar* ("men with wolf's skin") seem to allude, serve only to aid, to affirm this metamorphosis, to impress it upon friends and frightened enemies..." (141)

Certain rites of transformation and magical means were used together in combination with war. In our modern world it may not be entirely practical to join the military. It is possible and in fact likely to achieve fury without real combat by simply being angry enough (or at least convincing yourself you are angry). It may not be easy at first to elevate one's self into a level of fury, but everyone can talk himself or herself into being mad and that is just a step away. Personal competitive combat will be our best outlet for experimentation and development.

Anger and Strife

The factor that makes the art of war the most difficult to master is that it is the one we cannot practice within the arena of its birth. And those that do don't often live long enough to tell us if they fully develop its benefits. On the other hand, however, one of the factors that make this possibly the easiest art to master is the fact that we experience a minor form of fury just about everyday. You know the feeling, someone cuts you off in traffic, someone doesn't do their share at work, you are forced to stand in line forever like cattle, or someone blames you for something you didn't do. In fact just reading these words probably affects you because you emotionally resonate and visualize a personal experience I just described. Your demeanor changes, your body temperature goes up, heart rate increases, the mind hones in. It is that simple to start the process. Anger is easy to release and difficult to control just like war itself. As Barbara Ehrenreich so aptly puts it, "If war is a "living" thing, it is a kind of creature that, by its very nature, devours us. To look at war carefully and long enough is to see the face of the predator over which we thought we had triumphed long ago." (238). We can never be sure, even in the best of times, that anger will not rear its ugly head. You could be having the best day in your life and turn furious because some idiot rains on your parade.

In lieu of war, a key factor in determining the potential of a combat to initiate a furious state of being would be the difficulty of the challenge and what is at stake. Human beings love strife. We thrive on overcoming hardship but that difficulty must be balanced. If we are facing a challenger that is clearly our inferior the chance of fury is reduced. We need to have a real threat of failure to increase the likelihood of proper excitation. We must have a tough challenger whom we believe we can defeat if we are at our best (meaning furious). Anger also plays a key role here even if we have to manufacture it for ourselves. It can fuel the fire of combat in a way not possible without it. Tensions created by the other drives that have not been alleviated can also help. Anxiety over the outcome of the conflict due to the resources at stake or the possibility of injury and death also contribute. We can imagine that the encounter is for real. This would be the best training method: to be able in our mind to make the situation deadly. Barring that we may have to fabricate some personal slight by the opponent or some other reason why they deserve to be defeated. They must be separated from the self and put in a category of the 'other' (challenging antagonist).

This does have its dangers. I explained earlier how defeating an opponent sometimes requires becoming like them. In addition, once achieved a state of fury is hard to come down from. There are many examples of berserkers raging into their own troops after killing the entire enemy. Even long after the battle these feelings of separation can linger. Our ancestors devised elaborate rituals to calm warriors down as they reenter normal life and Rick Fields describes one of them with "The triumphal arch under which armies pass is thus a rite not so much of victory as of return from the exalted state of battle frenzy to the ordinary human state of civil society." (65). Many times in the past a society would offer their woman to returning soldiers in order to redirect their stored up energy.

Real Combat

There are many situations in which a person could engage in real combat. By real combat I am talking about a situation in which failure could result in death or serious injury. If we are looking to achieve fury then real life threatening situations offer some advantages. The advantage of real combat is the strength of the self-preservation and predatory instincts combined (death drive). When confronted with a true life-or-death situation the chemical reactions and bodily changes happen without much real effort on the part of the individual. Add in a little anger or strong hatred and the mix is volatile. This 'hatred' is one of the ways esses overtake the average person and can even override the elite warrior's personal aim for war if he or she is not careful. In *The English Warrior from Ancient Times to 1066*, Stephen Pollington explains:

> "In order to bring warriors to the point where they are willing to tackle, fight and kill other men, it is necessary to establish two conditions: the warrior must know himself to be a member of a group to whom he owes great loyalty by virtue of kinship, or common traditions, or common language, or whatever; and he must believe his enemy to be wholly outside this group, an 'alien' who poses a threat to the existence, property or freedom of the group, and against whom it is therefore legitimate to use violence as a means of thwarting these ambitions." (170)

It may be necessary to establish these conditions because our instinct to conquer is strong but not always our desire to kill vs. just defeat an opponent. With these ingredients, though, fury is almost a forgone conclusion of combat even for the average person. I say 'almost', because another possible reaction is flight. One other major consideration when faced with real danger is the reaction to fear. It can be a great trigger for fury or it can cause a paralyzing of action. Fear is also one of the easiest emotions to arouse in people whether we want to admit it or not. Fear is a great motivator and manipulator. The armies of the past learned this lesson well. Controlling morale was a big part of the strategy of warfare. Commanders needed to make sure they had the soldiers ready to kill and at the same time immune to or at least able to harness their fear. Mircea Eliade in Code of the Warrior explains one of the ways they countered this fear response,

> "'The essential part of the military initiation consisted in ritually transforming the young warrior into some species of predatory wild animal. It was not only a matter of courage, physical strength, or endurance, but of a magico-religious experience that radically changed the young warrior's mode of being. He had to transmute his humanity by an access of aggressive and terrifying fury that made him like a raging carnivore. ...in short, he no longer felt bound by the laws and customs of men.'" (61).

The motivation to run must be resisted and its energy turned to action. Some people define courage as 'not being afraid' but the truth is courage is 'being afraid but doing it anyway'. The warrior elite understands this principle and puts it to good use. Coupled with the confidence gained from training and success it is a near unbeatable combination.

The old *mannerbund* (men's bands) and secret societies are reflected in today's special operations forces. They have their own way of thinking, doing, and being. Special operations are ones in which a small force of highly trained and motivated individuals attack and defeat a much larger well entrenched opponent. William H. McRaven does a remarkable job of illuminating special operations in his book *Spec Ops: Case Studies in Special Operations Warfare: Theory and Practice*. He says "The key to a special operations mission is to gain relative superiority early in the engagement. ...relative superiority is a condition that exists when an attacking force, generally smaller, gains a decisive advantage over a larger or well-defended enemy." (6). This 'decisive advantage' starts well before the actual combat. It begins in the cult like conditioning and transformation of the warrior.

Special forces also require a different mindset in combat, one we will address later. Suffice it to say here the normal state achieved during life and death struggles in close quarters is a blind, unthinking, uncontrollable fury typically accompanied by a shutting down of certain senses. It is possible the spirit is unleashed on the objective world, a veritable 'Hel on wheels'. It also results in superior focus of effort to one aim (destruction of the enemy). Fury is the altered state of being achieved by an elevation of consciousness normally achieved through combat and causes heightened physical abilities with a dulling of sensation and thought. It is achieved through anger and violent activity in situations driven by mortido, libido, and physis. A blocking out or separation from the objective realm happens. Only the enemy exists and his destruction is necessary to reenter the normal reality.

Competitive Combat

Fury is possible in non-life threatening situations but it takes great effort to achieve it and substantial work to do so on a regular basis. Although not as easy to reach as it might be under life threatening conditions you will certainly have more opportunities to try. This happens for two reasons. One: civilized society limits availability and has rules against deadly encounters. Secondly: because of the nature of deadly encounters you may not survive long enough to develop an intimate relationship with fury. Don't be overly concerned, though, fury is just as much a part of non-leathal conflict. Robert Eisler suggests a possible reason why in *Man Into Wolf*:

> "Even today war combines two elements in it. One is the duel. This is the humanized development of animal' sexual fights, the only fighting which nature permits within the species.' ('Nature permits' is, of course, a mythological way of describing the facts simply as they are.) 'The fighting itself, the more it is studied, the more it shows itself to be far more a test of strength and endurance, of courage and will than of murderous and treacherous violence'... 'outstanding physiological weapons - horns though deadly against another attacking species such as the carnivores - lock against each other, cancel out as weapons in the sex-duel and so permit strength to be displayed with minimal damage." (221)

The 'sex-duel,' as he calls it, is a mix of drives, utilizing both the death drive and sex drive. The argument could be made it works with all three including the growth drive.

This sex-duel advantage augments the other advantages of competitive combat over real conflict. Without the anxiety of deadly encounters it will be easier for the Supra-conscious State to combine elements of the other states of being (ecstasy and exaltation). That is why we will select this competitive method as our art to develop while keeping real life threatening situations in mind as our focus during training. Competitive combat such as kickboxing, kung fu, and jiu-jitsu are prime examples, the more realistic the competition the better. Some of the full contact mixed martial arts events would be best because they most simulate real physical confrontations and do carry the potential for life-threatening injuries. The degree of excitement and violence in these events achieves levels most nearly equal to deadly encounters. As such they will also benefit the individual warrior should a real attack occur. This adds to the confidence and belief in one's self, which cannot be over emphasized. Point sparring is not recommended because it is too difficult to have that kind of control, low risk, and delicate placement of attack and still achieve the necessary excitation for fury to occur. The same is true of fencing and kendo, which is why they are not mentioned along with hand-to-hand skills. Here again, we are trying to discuss the most efficient ways of achieving fury.

Eisler makes another great point when he says "To abolish 'blood-sports' by legislation in this country may be possible. But the shortsighted sentimentalists who advocate it do not realize with what a terrific force the suppressed energies would break out elsewhere." (199). Man needs a place to vent these repressed energies. The section on drives touches on the need to express them in a manner conducive to their release and the potential problems if not properly vented. In fact it is quite possible the whole evolution of war occurred because we moved from predation practices (both as hunter and hunted) to agrarian culture and from the 'barbaric' non-lethal mano-a-mano sex-duel to the techno-stealth bomber.

War as it stands now may very well be the misguided venting of those frustrations. We have the non-initiated fighting over political aims instead of the warrior elite fighting for his own. In his research into the evolution of the warrior's code Rick Fields says:

> "And that, perhaps, is the underlying message of the first warrior. He might kill for many reasons, many of them inexplicable or even reprehensible to our eyes. He might kill for revenge, or to be admired, or to take a head to gain a powerful soul, or to give his child a name; in some cases he might even kill, like us, for resources like land or "protein." But whatever the causes of his fight, whether it had to do with the mythic-psychic undergrowth of the first planters,

or the ecological success of the fittest and fiercest, whether brave or chivalrous or sneaky, the first warrior's fight was personal. No one fought for him and no one could order or force him to fight." (34)

And as such he was the one who benefited most from the battles he won, and lost.

Unarmed, Melee, and Ranged

There are three main types of combat to be addressed. Unarmed combat is any conflict where the combatants use only the natural weapons of the body; hands, feet, head, knees, elbows etc. Melee combat is the use of hand held weapons such as swords, knives, and clubs. Ranged combat would include thrown weapons (stones, knives, etc.), bows and, of course, guns. They are listed here in order of value and usefulness for our purposes.

Unarmed combat is the most useful to us due to the amount of tension that can be released and the resulting feedback that cannot be matched by any other form. Melee is valuable especially for women, since it adds an element of destruction not possible with hands and feet. Women seem to have certain propensity for violence that manifests in throwing things. They seem to be especially adept at it. While it is possible to achieve and express fury with the use of ranged weapons (especially thrown ones) it is not recommended due to the low probability, the lethality discussed earlier, and other factors to be discussed later. Another reason to stay away from forms that require the use of weapons is practicality. In our society is it not possible to carry around weapons so their real life applications are limited.

If we are going to spend time walking the warrior path we might as well make the time as valuable as possible. Unarmed in this case is the only realistic choice. It solves all of our needs. It is the form of combat most likely to succeed in reaching a furious state. It is the form that adds the most confidence to the individual. It is the form that most effectively works out the physical body. It is also the weapon we can carry with us at all times. We 'never leave home without it' so to speak. It is also the form most likely to enable us to transform ourselves. We have seen this idea of transformation elsewhere in our quest and it will come up again and again. We want to maximize our effort and utilize our time as efficiently as possible so we may reach the zenith of power in our own physical lifespan. By mastering the Dark Arts of Immortality you will become a different Being.

Men and Women

Throughout history it appears that men have a markedly higher propensity for violence than do women. We have been given this idea that men are destructive and women are all nurturing. Don't be lulled into a false assumption. Men are just more physically and mentally developed to enacting violence. Women can be just as predatory and self-preserving as men. Obviously, women grew up in the same nature crucible as men and therefore faced the same challenges and threats. With their smaller stature and strength it shows that they indeed have a more powerful sense of purpose and self-preservation. Aside from the simple fact that women are here there is certainly evidence to support this theory of strong women beyond the myths of the Amazons. There is the Rus (pre-Russian area) women found on the battlefield described by Cedrenus, and there are many Norse sagas that speak of women warriors in full armor going into the fray. We already had our discussion of the Valkyrie and coincidently the areas mentioned also happen to be near the ancient territory of the Harii.

Women and men have similar drives with regard to war, they just exhibit them in ways more suited to their individual gender physiology, psychology, and pneumatology. That is not to imply that women are not capable of cultivating fury as well as men, it just means the methods may be slightly different. Women have an emotional advantage that does make up for the lower physical capability to enact violence. Men still have the edge when it comes to personal combat. However, certain principles may be applied to give the trained Dark Artist woman an advantage over the herd mentality males. Special operation forces' tactics could apply equally well in training one individual to beat a stronger one as they do with small units defeating larger armies. Even though men have some advantages in this art, the scales will tip in the other direction when we get to the art of sex and reaching the state of being, ecstasy.

Training and Style

There are really only three possible combinations in combat, A attacks & B defends, B attacks and A defends, or both A and B attack. If both parties defend then there really is no combat. So, what is an attack? When we break it down, each attack should be an attempt to kill the opponent with a single blow. There really is no better purpose for an attack. Although we could say incapacitate instead of kill. If your aim is just to stop your opponent and survive the encounter there is no reason the enemy has to die to satisfy those conditions. When we speak of defense there really is only one. Ultimately defense should be to avoid being hit. Therefore, the best attacks to study are ones that disable the opponent, and the only defense to master is evasion. Blocking is not a defense (except in melee combat with a shield or weapon). In unarmed combat evasion should be the only defense. Blocking is still being hit, and trapping in order to execute a counter is really an attack.

The importance of selecting the right style cannot be overstated. Many factors should be taken into account. It should consider (but not be limited to) your body type, age, effectiveness in life threatening encounters, and efficacy at unleashing full fury, etc. After evaluating these factors it is time to create a book of techniques to practice. Keep it simple. Plan out different encounters and situations and the various reactions to each. The most important thing to consider is the type of opponent. An untrained opponent is fought differently than a trained one. Size is the next consideration since an opponent smaller than you should be fought differently than an opponent twice your size. Analyze the attacks and defenses useful for each that matches your particular capabilities. Each move should be executed repeatedly with control until it becomes automatic. That way the perfection of the move will not deteriorate with heightened emotional content. Practice this style over and over and over. Then introduce high levels of anger through visualization, self-talk, etc. so you can most closely match real situational energy.

Here is a simple example of a stand-up (striker) fight strategy:

Lead arm: thumb/finger jab to eye, straight jab to throat. Lead elbow: close in hook to jaw. Rear arm: straight punch jaw, uppercut to jaw, hook to jaw. Rear elbow: close in uppercut to jaw. Head: butte nose. Lead leg: Snap kick groin, stomp lead foot. Lead knee: knee to groin. Rear Leg: round kick lead knee, rear spin kick to stomach. Rear knee: knee to xyphoid process.

This is a very simple but effective list of attacks. You should always use a combination of two, three or even four together on every attempt. Never strike once unless you have completely mastered all the Dark Arts. If you combine this with quick footwork you should come out pretty good in most encounters. Keep in mind it is necessary to incorporate some grappling tactics to complete this example and round out your striking ability. The same rules apply. You want to administer incapacitating techniques (joint breaks, chokes) at the same time you are evading those same techniques.

If you have trained in some martial art style don't get too cocky. I once saw a black belt in judo get beaten by a beginner in jiu-jitsu in less than a minute (five times in a row). Some black belts are near professional level fighters and some are worse than untrained couch potatoes. It depends on the person and the school. In general a martial artist striker (stand up style like boxing, kung fu, karate, etc.) will win about 95% of encounters with untrained individuals. The average person is not used to taking painful, trauma inducing blows so their will to fight falters rapidly. The shock of an initial blow is usually enough to wither most untrained people. This percentage would probably drop to 50% against an experienced street fighter or trained opponent. If we calculate in a skilled grappler (i.e. Brazilian jiu-jitsu stylist) they will probably win all encounters against an untrained opponent and 95% against a street fighter or striker martial arts stylist. The upright fighter is typically incompetent in grappling and nearly all, real and street fights go to the ground or at least a clinch. The odds are 50/50 against one of their own ilk. Obviously the whole equation goes out the window with a skilled mixed martial arts practitioner who combines both upright and ground fighting capability. A masterful striker/grappler is a walking lethal weapon.

McRaven's book on special operations is a perfect guide for developing a personal combat philosophy. Since his work deals with a smaller force defeating a larger, its principles should be doubly effective for a fighter attacking a similar sized opponent if we can utilize his ideas on 'relative superiority'. He explains, "To achieve relative superiority, the practitioner of special operations must take account of the principles [simplicity, security, repetition, surprise, speed, and purpose] in the three phases of an operation: planning, preparation, and execution." (9). Planning we have touched on already. Preparation means conditioning, training, being, etc. Execution speaks for itself. The principles of simplicity, security, repetition, surprise, and speed will be modified for use in unarmed combat theory, training, and use.

Simplicity is keeping to the best but minimum of techniques. We want to perfect them and the more techniques you have the less perfect they will be and it may take too long to choose or react with the appropriate response in a real fight. Security could easily be called intelligence because what we want to do is know as much about the enemy as possible while divulging little or no information about ourselves. Some information can be gathered ahead of time if it is someone you know or a specific type of preplanned confrontation. Other things can be picked up on through body language, such as fighting experience (we always recognize one of our own), style, size, and relative strength. Keeping these elements about yourself secret or hidden or using misinformation helps increase your odds of success. Repetition is doing it over and over again until the action comes without thought. The only way to get good at fighting is to fight. It relates to our discussion of microseconds and seeing fast things. The more you fight the more you can see techniques being used and to anticipate the most likely follow up attacks. Speed is paramount both in attack and defense. You must be able to avoid being struck but at the same time be able to deliver your own attacks at will. Again this only comes with practice. Surprise comes in two forms. One is feinting to misguide your opponent's attention. Two is attacking in such a way it causes a delay in his response. Delay is the most useful and is usually accomplished by attacking in ways the opponent does not expect, or with techniques he is not familiar with. Purpose is that for which you fight. Although survival of yourself or protection of a loved one would top the list, a desire for personal immortality should do the trick as well.

These are some of the practical elements of fighting. Do not lose sight of the fact the art of war's primary purpose is to teach you to experience fury on a regular basis. Put together the elements of anger, anxiety, and a powerful antagonist. By controlling fear, harnessing anger, and placing yourself into highly charged situations repeatedly you should develop a deep understanding of how to induce this state of being regularly. Once this degree of intimacy happens it will be easier to combine it with the supra-consciousness of ecstasy and exaltation. Remember the three necessary ingredients are a high degree of anger, anxiety over the outcome of the conflict, and a challenging opponent. Now get out there and fight.

IX. Art of Sex

*The seducer knows that people are waiting for pleasure -
they never get enough of it from friends and lovers,
and they cannot get it by themselves.*
- ROBERT GREENE

Ah, fucking! If there is a better activity on the planet for a human being I have never experienced it nor heard anyone talk of it. It is without a doubt the most remarkable process in the evolution of nature or the most incredible artistic creation of the divine. Sex has changed the world more than any other single practice. It rivals even war in this capacity because many times the fighting is over the possibility for sex. It exceeds even magic when it comes to harnessing the will toward its achievement. Men and women will go to nearly any length, risk any danger, throw away any possession to receive its secret pleasures. It runs the spectrum from the depths of depravity to the heights of spiritual union. But a key element of sexual experience that has been overlooked as a tool for human development is the supra-conscious state of being called ecstasy.

Not only is this art just as important as the other two it is arguably the most enjoyable and difficult at the same time. The art of sex is an extension of the sex drive and here we will guide it to a state of ecstasy. The sex drive is incredibly strong and it builds up a lot of tension when not released, especially in men. It is however the drive most likely to alleviate some of the tensions created by the other drives (mortido, physis). There is much more to this experience than mere procreation and pleasure as Crystal Dawn and Dr. Flowers say in *Sexual Alchemy: A Sado-Magical Exploration of Pleasure, Pain and Self-Transformation* with the following passage:

> "Who can deny the supernatural power of sex? Whether we see it as a conduit of the regeneration of life itself, or as a way to commune with the spirit and soul of another, or as a method of gaining power over another - the whole subject sparkles with the aura of magic. Sexuality is the most abundant basic power-source available to most human beings, and so harnessing it holds out the greatest promise for an abundance of magical power." (3).

There really is no banned sexual fetish as long as it is enacted between two or more consenting adults. Let me say that again. I am not condoning any activity with a minor or unwilling participant. Everything I refer to is strictly between consenting adults. I am simply saying that those two consenting adults could consent to anything with each other. In fact the use of fetishes is encouraged. This entire section is intended for adults only, and all descriptions and references refer only to acts performed between consenting adults.

Sex, like combat and magic, must be trained for with diligent attention but at the time of use it must be natural and without thought. The altered state of being achieved here is one of rapturous pleasure, the body wracked with spasms and followed by ultimate relaxation. This is a good experience, but obviously not welcome in all situations (can you imagine shopping for groceries in this condition). Fantasy and imagination are the ways to achieve it; sex is the way to drag it into the Objective world. It is a taste of the divine, a release of constraint, a true freedom of the senses. This is probably the most difficult art to master because it involves more variables than the other two. Sex is already pleasurable and to move it from something good to something great takes a different level of effort. Work that most people are too lazy, too self-conscious, or too guilt ridden to perform. It is a natural tendency to relax when things are good and it is very uncommon to work to make it great. Good is good enough, some might say. Sex is already a good thing (for those getting any) but it will need to be great in order to reach ecstasy. The key elements needed are passion for the target, anticipation of the pleasure, and fantasy fulfillment. You need mastery to be an artist at sex because you will have to deliver the experience for others and be able to achieve ecstasy for yourself. The driving forces behind ecstasy are love and lust. Either or both must be utilized to achieve the desired state. A great amount of desire must be incorporated into the selection of the partner to maximize the chance of ecstasy. It requires the proper balance of planning and spontaneity coupled with a build up of anticipation before the climax.

Ecstasy

There are several elements necessary to achieve the state of ecstasy. Desire and passion are among them and that makes it necessary to choose the correct target for your affection. The more challenging the hunt, or the more anticipatory the encounter, the more likely the outcome will result in ecstasy. It is most common for men and women to experience ecstasy at the point of orgasm. As Dr. Flowers points out in *Fire and Ice,*

> "...the orgasm has at least two levels of meaning. First, it is a physiological, and hence psychological, mechanism of energy release. (The magical value of this alone is very great.) Second and more importantly it is a manifold and multifaceted magical-symbolic "substance" in the form of a powerful sensation [pneumatological]." (188)

This statement really shows the tripartite nature of the orgasm and ecstasy. Women frequently reach an ecstatic state well before or immediately following orgasm as well, which creates a large window of opportunity. It is unfortunate that most men do not take advantage of this window to pleasure women. Due to the brief nature of the male orgasm and man's more diluted emotional capacity he is at a slight disadvantage when pursuing this art.

Ecstasy is a state of intoxicating pleasure. Sensory input is heightened to a preternatural level and experienced as a blissful release. Time distends. Sights, sounds, and smells overwhelm the mind and spirit. This perception is counter to the dulled sensory reception of fury and exaltation. It has the disadvantage of a loss of motor control that it shares with exaltation and a reduced awareness it shares with fury. It is important to get control of this facet of the Dark Arts. It will bring perceptive capabilities and happiness to even mundane tasks once mastered. Once the state is reached there is a skewed perception of time which all three states of being share to one degree or another.

There are some differences between the sexes when it comes to this area of work. I am talking here of heterosexual genders. This book is not trying to ignore homosexuality. They can certainly benefit from the practice of the Dark Arts; it is just not an area of experience that can be commented on easily. There is not as much available information on them, especially as it relates to historical and mythical involvement. From the perspective of evolutionary psychology most gay men view the world as a man and most gay women view the world as a woman. The facts seem to bare this out. Gay men are still visual and promiscuous while gay women are auditory and tend toward bonding and support. It appears our brains are based on genetics but our sexual predilections are not. Each homosexual will need to read the following data and evaluate which gender characteristics most closely match.

I am not trying to pigeonhole the sexes into one methodology but it is good to play the odds. This is my version of the 80/20 rule (not an exact ratio, more of an estimation). For example 80% of men appreciate looks vs. the 20% who rank it lower on their requirements for a mate. Eighty percent of men like having multiple sexual partners vs. the twenty percent who prefer a committed relationship. Eighty percent of women want a committed relationship and

80% want a spouse to provide good material support. When you start paying attention to things of this sort you will see so many areas of your life where the 80/20 rule applies.

My point is that if women generally like X then why not try X first with your woman until you find out her individual preferences. For example most men (about 95%) are turned on watching two lesbians and like the idea of engaging in relations with bi-sexual women. Even if you aren't a bisexual woman you could use this knowledge to your advantage. Women on the other hand have a totally different view of homosexuality. They don't typically find two men together appealing and it often has quite the opposite effect. Most women love erotic talk in bed. So a man who wishes to stand out from the rest should cultivate this ability. It is a known fact that most women are auditory while men tend to be visual. A man is turned on by what he sees and woman by what she hears or reads. This does not mean any old swear word will do. They are listening for sensual, erotic, sometimes even dirty talk but not foul. Outside of the bedroom the use of words goes even farther for women. If you constantly reassure a woman of her beauty, make her feel loved, and let her know she is accepted, as is, with your words you will be rewarded in abundance with respect and admiration. In other words (no pun intended) comfort her with proper words and reinforcing actions and she will pay you back in the bedroom.

Men tend to be more visually oriented. Sit down in any public area where women pass by and you can see this quite clearly as the men's heads turn like spectators at a tennis match. Women tend to be more auditory and feeling oriented. An easy way to find our for sure which preference the person has is to listen to them talk. If they use a lot of words like see, color, bright, they are probably visual. If they use words like hear, sounds, or loud they are auditory. If they use words like hot, cold, hard, feel, then they are kinesthetic (feeling oriented). To best communicate with that person, appeal to their modality by choosing similar words in your conversations with them and by leaning toward emotional phrases with women and thinking concepts with men. This works great in all long-term relationships and for building quick rapport.

Women have an emotional and physical advantage over men in achieving ecstasy. Their emotional advantage comes into play because strong emotions help reach ecstasy. Women naturally need emotional content in sex so they are already half way there. The other advantage is the number and length of times they can perform sex. The pleasure for women derived during the act of sex can reach extreme levels before orgasm. The fact they can reach orgasm multiple times and for an extended time also makes ecstasy more likely to occur. Unfortunately, most women have trouble finding a lover that can deliver the goods. Some reach orgasm only rarely and never experience the heightened pleasure beforehand needed to reach ecstatic experience.

Men on the other hand have the advantage of nearly always reaching orgasm. Unfortunately they can select partners and perform sex without the emotional connections so they don't always have the emotional content needed to reach ecstasy. Men suffer from another disadvantage because once they reach orgasm they generally need a recovery period and the length of orgasm is very short, limiting the opportunity for extended pleasure and ecstasy. These biases all have their exceptions and variations. The idea is to find out as much as you can before hand, to play the odds, or do both.

Lust and Love

A necessary ingredient to experiencing ecstasy is a high level of desire. Passion burns in the blood and under the right circumstances its fuel can ignite fires that burn the world. Another area of difference typical of the sexes is the contrast between lust and love. It is not an either/or issue but the degree of each is pretty universal. Men typically have a higher level of lustful feelings and love is secondary (if it exists at all). Most men would probably agree that they are not searching for someone to fall in love with but if the woman falls in love with him that is ok. With regard to love men are more often prey than predator, it is unfortunate that we recognize it too late in most cases. Women, on the other hand, typically have a tremendous capacity for love and lust falls secondary. They appear to always be searching for that elusive sublime romance. Women love to fall in love and will often even delude themselves in order to allow those emotions free reign. Kreidman explains,

> "A woman falls in love because of the way she feels about herself when she's with you. From her point of view, she needs to believe you are constantly thinking of her and that you are counting the moments until she will be in your arms again. This may be only a fantasy for her, but with a little effort from you, it can come true. You, too, can join the ranks of great lovers, those men who are able to turn a woman's fantasy into reality." (15, 26).

It is the 'fantasy' element of love though that gives women their power. Someone summed it up for me pretty succinctly by saying men give love to get sex and women give sex to get love. We each need what we need and these two elements in whatever combination within the individual can move mountains.

The higher the levels of passion the more likely the sexual encounter will result in ecstasy. The importance to you is for you to decide which proportion of fuel is necessary for you to fire ecstasy. It is also helpful to understand the other genders perspective so you can appeal to it in seductive attempts. Lust and love are both related to libido (sex drive) and in the instance of love possibly physis (the growth drive). Within the context of immortality through progeny it is possible to connect mortido (death drive). We don't want these powers to control us but for us to gain control of them. That doesn't mean to squelch them but to harness them to our own ends with full understanding.

Love has taken on an almost spiritual air and maybe rightly so. Its primary qualities are attraction, devotion, and admiration. A man or woman in love will do nearly anything to gain the attention of the target of their attraction. They will also do nearly anything to acquire that affection in return. It may in fact be one of the most antinomian emotions in the human repertoire. As Young defines it "Love... is something so subtly insane that only humans are clever enough to fall into it." (102). Although it is the most widely covered word in literature it still remains an enigma. It is almost impossible to get a complete definition. It falls back to the experience situation I mentioned in a previous section. I liken it to the supreme courts ruling on pornography. They said 'if asked to define it, they could not, but they know it when they see it'. Anyone who has experienced love knows it through and through, but probably could not fully articulate the spell they were under at the time.

Love is certainly an admirable emotion but up until the Troubadours in the 12th century it did not connote the higher spiritual nobleness it has come to be associated with now. In ancient times it was closer to the word *eros*. Eros is lust. Lust is a purely sexual desire for union with the target of that attraction. Where love is a more spiritual and emotional passion, lust is more related to physical pleasure and possession. Lust is a valuable emotion to fire the libido. If it is also tied to love for the same person great, but lets be realistic. Your most pleasurable sexual encounter was likely not with the person you loved the most. Lust is especially powerful when directed at someone we don't have but think it is possible to acquire. There is an unmistakable chemistry between compatible lovers. Heights of ecstasy need lust and for women maybe love as well.

Fantasy

One of the hardest things to do is make something good, great. There are plenty of good athletes but few great ones. There are plenty of good restaurants but few great ones. There are plenty of good lovers but few great ones. It is a normal tendency in people to relax once something reaches good. Plus the work involved to get over the hump (no pun intended) from good to great can be considerable. One of the main ways to make sex great and not just good is through the use of fantasy fulfillment. The fantasy can be as simple as seducing someone thought to be out of reach or as complex as doing it in the elevator of the Eiffel tower during the first winter snowfall. Jacobi says "Jung attaches great importance to the creative activity of fantasy, which he even puts in a category of its own, because in his opinion in cannot be subordinated to any of the four functions [thinking, feeling, sensation, intuition], but partakes of them all." (24).

Fantasy is where the art of sex can truly become an artistic expression. It is an act of creation, maybe *the* act of creation for the mind. Sarah Worth says it well in her essay *Paradox of Real Response to Neo-fiction* with "When engaging with fiction we do not *suspend a critical faculty*, but rather *exercise a creative faculty*. We do not actively suspend disbelief - we *actively create belief*."[4] It has been proven over and over again that the mind cannot always tell the difference between the real and the imagined. If you doubt the power of creative visualization just try this. Picture a big slice of lemon. Feel its cool skin in your hand, the wetness as the juice slowly oozes over your fingers. Now raise the lemon slice to your mouth and take a big bite. Did your mouth salivate and your jaws clench?

Fantasy satisfies a great need and is part and parcel of the human condition. It is a function of dreams and aspirations. Nothing is more pleasing to humans than the satisfaction of those dreams. As Robert Greene puts it in *The Art of Seduction*, "What people lack in life is not more reality but illusion, fantasy, play." (xxiii). Reality beats people to a pulp. You can save them from this by giving them their fantasy, and if you want to rejuvenate your love of life satisfy your own. Don't feel that you are crazy because of the fantasies you hold. Don't over-analyze them either. We are not here to figure out why you want what you want, just how we can harness it to your own ends. Another way to benefit personally from fantasy is to act out a fantasy for your partner. Pleasing a partner can be a most rewarding sexual encounter and can lead to ecstasy for both (or all) participants.

Be sure you consider all the elements of your fantasy. Primarily think about the situation and setting. Engaging all the senses can also help ease the transition to a higher state of consciousness. Be sure if you don't enhance

---

[4] *Ibid (184)*

a sensory experience to at least not make it worse. It is ok to avoid scented candles and incense but make sure if you do there aren't any offensive odors in the vicinity (that includes yourself). The same goes for music. It is ok to want it quiet, but make sure background and street noises won't intrude. Another way to ruin a good fantasy is to be disappointed because it did not live up to your expectations. If your expectations are too high and the moment does not satisfy them it can be devastating. Anticipation is paramount for achieving ecstasy through fantasy but caution needs to be taken here as well. If you drag it out too long it can become a frustration. Don't overdue your anticipation or expectation, let the moment unfold how it will and just enjoy it. You don't want to forget the antinomian nature of taboo either. Make sure you find elements you consider 'naughty' to be included. Fantasy is the best way to bring the will into the game of love and lust.

Preferences

Understanding your own sexual preferences helps with the general practice of building opportunity for ecstasy. Every time you have sex, which is hopefully a lot, is not always going to present the opportunity for fantasy fulfillment or ecstasy. People like to think sex needs to be spontaneous and to an extent that is ok. But don't let the idea lull you into bad habits. Too often individuals think that fate or destiny is in control of love and romance. They think things will just fall into place when they meet the right person. Nothing could be further from the truth. If you want love and romance you will have to create it for yourself and the target of your affection. There is something to be said for chemistry but don't leave everything else up to chance. What I just said about love and romance applies equally well to sexual practice itself. Ecstasy is not going to just fall into place. It requires work on your part. Every sexual encounter offers an opportunity for improvement in your skills but not always an opportunity for altered consciousness and elevated being. Don't ruin it with too much thought but don't allow those too few chances to go to waste either. Create a nice balance. Practice techniques regularly and attempt ecstasy occasionally when the moment is right.

One issue that will come up sooner or later is to stay with one lover or to have many. Since in most cultures the accepted practice is monogamy the antinomian standpoint would be to explore polygamy; likewise in the rare polygamous culture, monogamy. Antinomian methods are meant to serve your aims but you don't have to become a slave to the idea. Go with your personal preference, the world be damned.

A monogamous relationship is both a blessing and a curse when it comes to the art of sex. It depends on the individuals. If there is a deep love between the people involved it can be easier to reach a blissful state during sex. If satisfying your partner is important to your own fulfillment you have the advantage of familiarity (as long as you don't take things for granted) so you will have a great deal of knowledge in that area. There is also the strong emotional bond that can be conducive to ecstasy. Opportunity to try out various fantasies normally not practical with a new relationship can be done in abundance with an adventurous partner. If your partner is agreeable, monogamy can enable you to try such things as sex-magical practices and unusual fetishes. You will have the time to improve and master old techniques and have the thrill of experimenting with new ones. Unfortunately long-term monogamous relationships usually result in a decline in sexual fervor. Routine sex becomes boring. If not properly tended to the opportunities for ecstasy will decline or disappear altogether.

Polygamy will tend to keep things ever changing but without the bond of a steady relationship it can result in dry spells. Polygamy seems especially appealing for men due in part to their emotional detachment and psychological evolution (biological preference for numerous short-term sexual relationships). It offers some other emotional advantages as well. By having multiple partners it is likely all your needs will be met. One partner or the other will satisfy certain cravings leaving you free of frustration and making it possible to enjoy the special moments with each lover. Sometimes one partner won't perform certain acts creating resentment and leaving you wanting. This can be a real problem in relationships and prevent ecstatic experience. If it is the excitement of conquest that you seek then monogamy will be a hindrance for you. Polygamy relies on utilizing primarily the power of lust. It will be best to pick a target that is difficult to acquire thereby raising the anticipation level during pursuit and the satisfaction gained through victory. Another simple advantage to this type of relationship is the possibility of satisfying only yourself. Alleviated from responsibility for a partner's pleasure can be a liberating experience of self-enjoyment and result in ecstasy. Take your pick, monogamy or polygamy, it is all good. Just understand which works best for you and consider the implications.

No work of this type would be complete without addressing some of the physical techniques of sexual pleasure. The two classics in the realm of sex practices are the *Kama Sutra* and *The Joy of Sex*. Techniques should be performed to engage the Objective, Subjective and Noujective worlds of each practitioner. Objective techniques include all manner of physical exploration and applications (oral sex, G-spots, A-spots, positions, other erogenous zones). Subjective techniques would include erotic talk, body language, costumes and suggestive anticipation. Noujective engagement beyond personal chemistry would require fantasy elements like bondage, S&M, ritual, locations, etc. There are so many fetishes out there you should investigate them for your self and try some at least once if not regularly. This is especially true if any cause a strong response from you. This will also help you to understand the personal preferences of others. To be a great lover you need to be accepting of your partner's predilections. Women especially need to feel it is ok to tell their mate anything and it will be accepted without judgment. So if your girlfriend mentions something about peanut-butter, big toes, and a tennis racket, it would be best if you smile suggestively and ask who serves first. In many cases you may need to figure out their fetishes for them so the more experience you have the better. As long as their desires don't totally repulse you, you should be willing to help enact them. The more open you are to anticipating these peculiar desires of others the better lover you become. The better lover you become, the more you will carry yourself in such a manner as to be recognized by other people. That recognition will lead to more opportunities and you know what that means. More sex, ahhhhh!

Seduction

This may be the most important section in this chapter. It is possible to use autoerotic practices like masturbation to reach ecstasy (especially due to the fantasy element). But let's be realistic, you cannot develop sex to an art form if you aren't getting any and the quality of experience is worthless (at least lacking) without the involvement of another adult. Ecstasy is much more likely to occur and exceedingly more useful if it is attained with another person's participation. You are not only satisfying your personal needs but also the needs of the other person. So go for it.

One of the first steps to being a great seducer is to get in shape. I have already discussed the need for fitness to practice the Dark Arts. I am sure you see the value for personal combat but that isn't the only reason. Fighting requires it, sexual performance needs it, and the pain techniques used in ritual magic will tax you in ways you never dreamed. It is especially helpful here to attract a partner. I am going to repeat it again. Contrary to political correctness: if you look bad, get off your ass. Start now. Put this book down and do ten push-ups, or go for a walk and come back to it. The better your body looks the more likely you are to get laid. Fact. Live with it. Beyond this are many keys to the puzzle.

Robert Greene identifies two of the most powerful elements needed in seductions when he says "Creating love and enchantment becomes the model for all seductions - sexual, social, political. A person in love will surrender." (xxi). 'Surrender' is what we want both for ourselves and for the target of our affection. There is really no way to know for sure what will work on any given individual but you can play the odds (80/20 rule). Men are visual and women are auditory. Women will be seduced easier with love and men with enchantment (lust). Although, don't count on only one method if it is possible to apply several. Just be sure to start with the one that has the highest probability of success in order to buy sufficient time to apply the others. Becoming a master at utilizing both in all seductions is the aim since it gives the greatest probability for success.

Some of the other pieces of the seduction puzzle are the three C's (Carry, Clothes, and Conversation). By carry I mean the body language message you present that others interpret (consciously or not). By clothes I mean your personal grooming and wardrobe. And by conversation is meant the way you speak and the words you choose. What you don't say can be as important, maybe even more so than what you do say. These are the first steps to becoming an adept seducer. They are used in all cases and by maximizing a style that best matches your personal strengths it will make you irresistible. Keep in mind to appeal to all five senses in your planning and execution.

The first one I will cover is carry. By this I mean how you carry yourself. The two things to be considered are how you move and the invisible air. An observer will read volumes about your character into how you stand and walk and move. They may not be accurate conclusions but people make them every day. The observer may not even know what it is they like or dislike about you and if asked probably couldn't describe it but body language can help or hinder your opportunities for seduction. You pick. Handle it consciously or not but either way it has its effect. It may be subliminally perceived and never even enter the conscious thoughts of the observer but it colors interaction none-the-less.

For attracting women a man needs to have a method of motion that is both commanding and graceful. As Ellen Kreidman explains in *Light Her Fire* "If you can combine the strength of a lion or tiger with the gentleness of a teddy bear or pussycat, if you can be as hard as a rock and as soft as drifting fog, you can become the most sought-after man on earth." (129). This duality is the very reason men fall into the 'friends' trap, and why the 'nice guy' doesn't get any. A woman wants both a good boy and a bad boy. Too much of either will ruin a seduction so try for a mix (bad good boy, or good bad boy). Walk with a strong upright posture without being stiff. Keep your head up and your shoulders back. If your pace is typically fast, slow down. A nice leisurely gate is best. Tell yourself you are not in a hurry to get where you are going. Women also see hands as sensual so when grasping or holding something use the same combination. Your movements should be sure yet slow and gentle.

For a woman to attract a man she needs to combine the walk of a virgin and a slut. Sounds like a similar duality doesn't it. Men love to think they are corrupting a good girl with their conquests. Walk with a pleasant serenity but combine it with hip movements that suggest sexual invitation. A sensual saunter is best combined with a sultry posture so as to suggest joy not aloofness, potential not professional. If you look stuck up and unapproachable men won't take the bait.

The air of confidence I am talking about is your ability to believe you can deliver the goods. Did you ever wonder why some people have no problem picking up lovers? They don't have money or looks and yet still score on a regular basis. It is because they operate in a certain way that tells people non-verbally they can deliver. It may not even be conscious on their part. It may be natural for them. This harkens back to the sections on will and hamingja in relation to charisma. People, especially women can detect this air. The best way to project this demeanor is to be a *great* lover, not just good. You do that by educating yourself and getting practical experience. There is no substitute for experience and the more knowledge you have going in the more likely you will maximize the value of the act itself.

If you can't deliver the goods you need to act as if you can. In fact you must learn to convince even yourself of this fact to pull it off well. Hopefully you can do this successfully long enough to actually become a great lover. Did you ever wonder why when you aren't dating anyone no one shows any interest in you? Why when you go to a party by yourself you generally remain that way and when you arrive with an attractive partner everyone in the place seems to be interested? The minute you have a good partner flirts fall out of the woodwork. It is because people can smell desperation and success a mile away. Women are masters of this intuitive radar. They are adept at sensing someone happy and complete and this is attractive to them. Everyone wants to be around someone desirable. To take command of this power you have to train yourself to carry that air of desirability even when you are alone and desperate, especially when you are alone and desperate, because that is when you are normally repelling people. In your mind you must plant the thought firmly you have an awesome lover at home waiting on you. As soon as you get done shopping, eating, drinking, whatever, you are heading straight home to be with them. You will be amazed how effective this technique is. If you learn only one thing about seduction make it this one!

The next factor to consider is clothing. There is an old saying 'Clothes make the man'. It applies to women as well. It isn't mandatory for you to go out and buy Armani or Liz Claiborne (but if you can afford it, go for it). The key here is to put your best foot forward all the time. You never know when you will be in a place to meet the person you are looking for. Don't wait until Saturday night clubbing to dress and groom your best. In fact you will have more success during mundane weekly activities. That is when the competition is lacking and people's defenses are down. It is also extremely intriguing and often taboo to have a seduction take place when and where you least expect it.

It really doesn't cost much to create a great look; it just takes some research and analyzing on your part. It is very important to have a stylish or unique appearance. Something that will get you a lot of attention is best. There are several well-written books on style and dressing to impress people. You can go to your local bookstore and look at books and magazines on clothing and hair for free. Advertisers are masters of clothing and getting attention so this is the one time you should pay attention to ads, billboards, and commercials. Don't do this for clothing commercials because of course they will portray their clothing well. Instead, pay attention to the actors in other types of commercials and think about the demographic of the audience. Is it the same as the demographic of your sexual target? Finding a great hairstyle can be done in the same way. Makeovers are big business and regularly appear as the subject of talk shows, which are another avenue of free research. Keep all five senses in mind when doing your planning. Personal cleanliness and grooming go hand in hand with clothing. Remember the fingernails and unwanted hair men. Not only is it a sign of personal cleanliness but also the discomfort these cause against a woman's skin can destroy their mood so they look for them immediately upon meeting you. Odor is another delicate area that needs to be addressed with appropriately chosen perfumes and deodorants. You don't want to completely destroy natural scent (pheromones), but you wish to eliminate offensive odors.

Another interesting source of information on this subject is Anton Szandor LaVey's book *The Satanic Witch*. He speaks primarily of methods of magical glamour and fascination using the principles of sex, sentiment, and wonder. Sex being obvious of course, sentiment related to reminding your target of something from their past, and wonder in relation to the more antinomian concept of standing out from the crowd by being a bit different. He frequently remarks on the nature of the taboo and the hidden in clothing selection. These are important topics we have discussed as well. Slightly revealing clothes get more seductive attention than blatant flaunting. Whatever your choice, unless you are creating a look to attract a specific person (or type) don't blend into the masses. The use of antinomian thinking here can be a great benefit to you and the target.

Conversation is the next piece to seduction. Some things to consider first are the distinctiveness of talking. This includes the tone, pitch, speed, and word selection. If you have an exotic accent because of foreign birth or exposure, great, use it. People find accents mysterious and exciting so play it up. If you are attempting a seduction in your country of origin then train yourself to speak the language perfectly. A simple example is how most people in America say "yea", "yup", or "ah-huh" instead of yes. This simple change in habit will bring amazing positive notice. Enunciate every word articulately, clearly, and naturally. Improve your vocabulary as much as you can. Don't attempt to dazzle people with big words, but find clear concise ways to use impressive language. Learn to use pitch and inflection, don't sound mechanical (unless trying to pick up an engineer). Did you ever notice how even in a loud room someone could get your attention with a whisper?

Effective conversation has many other elements that can be the focus of further study on your part. Humor is the best weapon of language you have in your arsenal. Learn it. Use it. Everyone loves to laugh because if feels good. People like to be around people that make them feel good. They are drawn to those individuals and want to be around them on a regular basis. Don't over do it or you won't be taken seriously as a lover. Proper balance is the key. Effective listening is another under utilized element. People tend to talk too much or listen too little when attempting a seduction. You must listen to what the other person has to say and to what they don't say. You cannot do this if you are thinking of what you want to say next and sitting poised for a pause in their talking. Ask questions and let the other person speak, especially about their own concerns. Don't make it an interview. Give and take but show a definite interest in what they have to say and let them do the bulk of the speaking (80/20). Even if you know more about the subject than they do, keep quiet. Showing them how smart you are will get someone else laid, not you. Intimacy comes not by telling them but by shutting up and letting them tell you. Use your knowledge to ask them intelligent questions about their passions. The more they talk the more they will consider you interesting (sounds counter-intuitive but trust me on this one).

The key to getting the opportunity to converse starts with being aggressive and a great flirt. There are many books on the topic of flirting and it will take some practice. The main point on flirting is to do it all the time. Flirting with someone you are not really interested in helps you perfect your skills. The better you are at flirting with an unattractive stranger the more comfortable and sincere you will sound during a real seduction attempt. Again this is not something you turn off and on. It must be up and running always. It will seem most natural and hence most effective when it is a part of who you are on a daily basis. Another great source of help comes from the sales profession. Get a book on selling and learn the techniques for building rapport and closing the deal for in a sense that is the goal of seduction. You are selling yourself.

The main focus of this chapter was the supra-conscious state of being called ecstasy. The art of sex is a large part of the triad of Dark Arts. Ecstasy brings the element of pleasure and increased sensory perception to the other powers gained through fury and exaltation. It is the reward for hard work. After all, everybody loves pleasure. Further discussions and techniques will help blend the abilities gained from all three states (see figure 7). Those techniques will help balance out the disadvantages and increase the advantages. Of all the arts I hope you spend a lot of time on this one. It is one of my personal favorites. So stoke up those fires of passion with the right target, savor the anticipation of pleasure, and fulfill those nasty little fantasies of yours.

X. Art of Magic

The subjective universe is capable of a full spectrum of possibilities which range from virtually absolute precisions to almost total delusion because it is not bound by natural laws.
-Dr. Stephen Flowers

The objective of the art of magic is to achieve the state of being we will call exaltation. Just as with fury and ecstasy the practice of magic does not guarantee the achievement of an exalted state but for our purposes it is the best method available. The practice of magic by its very nature is antinomian, and is a direct training and expression of the will. The exalted state of being allows us to view the Universe and our particular world manifestations in a different way. The awareness level achieved is more all pervasive and encompassing. Magic has been replaced by science in the modern world but it is time to reclaim its power. As Dudley Young says,

> "But science, having progressed by eschewing the magical as primitive and childish, has tempted us also to forgo the magical in our pursuit of the world-soul. This simply cannot be done: if you want to traffic with the invisible, you have to use magic. Because we have forgotten this, particularly since the Renaissance, we are in many respects more ignorant of *pneuma's* desires than were our primitive forebears." (xxvii)

And 'trafficking with the invisible' is exactly what we want to do.

There are many definitions of Magic. The classical definition was coined by Aliester Crowley and was basically 'causing change to occur in conformance with will.' When he said this, he meant making something happen that would not have ordinarily happened without the use of willing. Change in the physical environment in conformance with will is a tall order. We have already discussed the use of action, speech, and will to make changes in the Universe and our own worlds. It is not a matter of selecting one method. It is about using all three methods in conjunction. As we can see from our understanding of how the Universe works, that magic and change are not just pure acts of will, and forcing direct effects in the Material dimension may be the least practical application of willing. As with capability it is best to know your own strengths and weaknesses. I go back to the discussion of ascribing abilities to your self you think you already have. We need to use will in all cases but especially when its power is most useful, hence self-transformation. Since will is tied to the invisible world (noujective), making changes to yourself with magical practices is much more effective and rewarding in the long run than attempting to bend a spoon. This doesn't lessen the need for willing in all activities it just points out the need to really focus when and where you gain the most benefit. The practice of magic itself is designed to strengthen the will; basically it is a form of exercise for will 'power'.

My definition of magic is a methodology whereby the will, guided by belief, augments or violates causality in accordance with one's intent. I already covered the problem of mental and spiritual functions being considered causal so here we have a strong reason to use magic to alter internal functions. Belief is all powerful or all limiting depending on what you hold to be true. Intent is what you want to happen when you perform some action or the message you wish to convey when you speak. Things don't always occur in line with your intentions. Will helps to enforce your intent upon the Universe's hidden dimensions.

In the above definition I am also referring to the causal relationship of the Material dimension. Magic is an attempt to reach beyond your own Objective world through the use of the invisible forces that surround us (possibly by influencing the Astral and Ethereal). Remember if you change your being in one dimension it affects the others, therefore if you change someone else's it does the same. In this case it could be considered causal, but we don't completely understand all the mechanisms involved so we will leave it at that.

Magical names are used to more identify with the whole self. You may think you are not a fractured being but how many times have you talked to yourself. If you were whole you would already know what you were going to say so why would you need to say it. You also have the core identity fighting with the memes that wish to control thinking. To bring the will into awakened consciousness takes a consistent effort. To join the warrior, lover, and mage requires extreme dedication. To facilitate this select a name that is aesthetically pleasing to you and assimilate that identity into the whole Self. This is kind of like starting with a clean slate. Through training and preparation, and the use of ritual, an exalted state is reached. Magical techniques are similar to martial and sexual ones. You must focus the mind and will when training. But when it comes to execution you don't concentrate too hard, you just let it happen. You must train yourself until it is automatic. Your power works your intent without attention, which is another reason to unify the self so there is no conflict of intent.

We are also going to put full control and power into the hands of the Self. No authority or power will be given over to some other individual, organization, or God. With that authority goes responsibility. Robert North points out the reason it is so easy to place power outside of our selves when he says,

> "Both of these formulae [inhibitory meditation and excitatory magicks] were very human responses to the feeling of alienation, the sense that humankind is a stranger on Earth, not evolved from it; placed here by some unknowable transcendent power that is distant yet familiar." (1)

Don't make the same mistake. This feeling can lead to a desire to subjugate one's self to a 'higher power', but do not give in. Our failure to achieve something will be our own doing. Accountability for the repercussions of our choices (or lack there of) will also be our own. Ascension is squarely in the hands of the individual. You either make it or you don't.

Exaltation

The definition of exaltation is an excessively intensified sense of wellbeing or importance. It also means to raise high, as in rank, power, or character. For our purposes it represents the primary expression of the growth drive (Physis). Arthur Lyons sees a similar concept in describing Anton's magic system in *Satan Wants You* stating

> "'Emotion,' or 'adrenal energy,' as LaVey calls it, is the cornerstone of his system of magic. His rituals, he has explained, were designed to induce in the celebrant a subjective state through which he or she might be able to summon and direct his or her own psychic powers to achieve external goals. This is not 'magic,' in the classic sense of invoking demonic entities and sending them out to do one's bidding, but the harnessing of one's own extrasensory biological powers - what LaVey calls 'applied psychology multiplied tenfold.'" (114)

We are accomplishing something similar by multiplying consciousness tenfold.

Physis and its relation to the magician should be clear enough. The mage is the archetypal philosopher/priest king. It is in his nature to quest for the hidden and unknown in his search for the secrets to personal power. In order to accomplish this feat requires the ability to see the Universe and him self in a different light. The magician breaks down his being and then rebuilds it so it is more conducive to sealing the schism in his psyche. It is this exalted state that allows us to see our worlds and the whole of the Universe from a unique perspective that allows for this reconstruction to be undertaken. The key elements needed to achieve this state are ambition, pain, and mystic ritual.

Exaltation generally results in a form of awareness and clarity of understanding expanded to preternatural levels. It is an overwhelming sense of one's self and personal identity in relation to the greater Universe (to include all three dimensions). For all that it elevates the Self, there is a corresponding relinquishing of bodily coordination and a dulling of the senses. Looking at figure 7 you can see the benefit derived (expanded awareness) and how it is at direct odds with the shared disadvantage of fury and ecstasy (narrowing of awareness). Exaltation brings higher awareness but shares its dulled senses with fury and its reduction of physical attributes shared with ecstasy. For its own sake it brings a level of awakening unattainable by other methods and results in a supra-consciousness that warps the perception of time. It shares this time warping with fury and ecstasy. Pain is the primary anchoring technique used in mystic ritual to keep connected to the Material dimension. Pain brings a sharpened awareness of reality in the Objective world slightly askew of normal perception. By experiencing the supra-conscious state of being, exaltation, on a repeated basis it will enable you to merge its benefits with the benefits of other states with none of the disadvantages. Exaltation fuels itself on the ambition of the mage.

Ambition

An extension of physis (growth drive) appears as the emotion of ambition and it aims at improving the individual as well as striving toward freedom. As Nietzsche puts it in *The Will to Power* (translation by Walter Kaufmann and R. J. Hollingdale):

> "'But this is the oldest and healthiest of all instincts; I should add, 'one must want to have more than one has in order to *become* more.' For this is the doctrine preached by life itself to all that has life: the morality of development. To have and to want to have more - *growth*, in one word - that is life itself.'" (77)

The black magician carries this desire to its natural apex. He wills himself to become a god (Divinely Ascended Immortal Soul).

In a direct way what we believe draws those things to us (for good or ill). Sometimes it runs counter to our intentions. For instance we might go to a party with the intent of having a good time. Unfortunately, on the drive over we believe it will be boring and socially uncomfortable. Sure enough you have a terrible time. Looking back on it objectively you will see that it was your belief that made it so. Having gone with a different attitude would have resulted in an entirely different experience. Belief can sabotage intent in many ways, or it can be the most powerful force behind every action. When belief agrees with intent it increases the likelihood of success. Again we could go back to the discussion of confidence and knowing you can deliver the goods. One of the main functions of magic was to be able to reshape your social and cultural programming and set new parameters of your own choosing. This can only happen with a belief system conducive to its attainment. Attitude is everything.

Another benefit of practicing magic is the fact that it extends life. Studies have shown that when people have control over difficulties and problems in their life even if they can't solve them they encounter less stress. Lower stress levels are proven to aid longevity. This reduction of perceived ineffectiveness to deal with an issue and reduction of stress results in longer life. Magic helps you live, longer. It provides control over the unseen forces affecting you. Bloom agrees with "Though it may be riddled with bizarre errors and ludicrous imagery, a vision of the unseeable [such as myth, religion, magic] produces some small fragment of real mastery." (132). Studies (physiological and psychological) show that when people have control over an issue it results in better health and happiness. If bad situations are forced on someone they suffer more and succeed less frequently than those people who sought out those challenges head on. Those who feel they have no control perform worse than those who feel they do, even if that control is an illusion.

Since magic gives you options and control normally not available, and opportunities to achieve things normally out of reach, it leads to a more balanced and longer life. Prayer acts in a similar way by giving the illusion of a solution to the problem when no other option is available. It is not as effective as magic, and in some cases not at all effective where magic would have been. Especially, since God isn't going to fix anything for you. Prayer relinquishes power to an outside agency so this does not help the individual fully capture the feeling of control. Black magic is already antinomian and presenting this image helps you throw off the societal repressions keeping you under control. This taboo is the antinomian aspect needed for self-deification.

Ritual and Pain

The first step you must undertake is to learn a system of magic. For the Germanic paradigm we are following in this work that would be runes, galdor, or seidhr. There are many systems of magic out there. Dr. Flowers explains the variation in *Hermetic Magic*,

> "Perhaps the most significant reason why magic can not be explained in the rational, predictable way some might wish is that the magicians are all *different*. Magic is the exercise of the will of an individual, and as such it is dependent on the state of being of that individual at the moment the magical operation is executed." (140)

This is the very same reason you should select a particular brand of magic on your own. I am not going to go into the basics of each one. It is up to you to match yourself to the appropriate system. Decide based on your cultural background, aesthetics, practicality, chance, or purely on whim. It really doesn't matter as long as you incorporate the elements of ambition, pain, and mystic ritual.

You have probably already worked on some system of magic. Now it is time to master it with the focus I will give you here. If you have not studied magic before do your own work in this area. Find a system that is appealing to you and which you think will help you hold a strong belief. Be warned; magic is the most difficult thing in the worlds to do well. The advantage for the beginner though is the near immediate results you will see in yourself. The other advantage is that you haven't wasted your time yet. *LaVey* cuts to the chase on this one in *The Satanic Bible* with the following, "The true magus knows that occult bookshelves abound with the brittle relics of frightened minds and sterile bodies, metaphysical journals of self-deceit, and constipated rule-books of Eastern mysticism." (21). You have not spent a lot of time practicing useless candle burning and rock collecting. Exaltation will actually be easier for you to reach since you won't have to un-condition yourself to a bunch of bullshit.

Whatever your chosen magical medium you need to add only three things to it. I have talked about ambition already. You must have a profound desire to achieve godhood and immortality. Second you must utilize pain. Third you must incorporate both into an antinomian-based ritual. Most magical systems miss at least one of these three elements. As such they all fail to obtain the results sought. For those of you experienced at magic here are the answers to why it didn't work. Incorporate these concepts and your success will be exponential.

Pain is the most commonly missed element in the practice of magic. In all the old systems it has become blurred by the elaborate claims of bloodletting and sacrifice. *LaVey* must have seen this as well since he says in *The Satanic Bible*:

> "Contrary to all established magical theory, the release of this [life] force is NOT effected in the actual spilling of blood. ...This discharge of bio-electrical energy is the very same phenomenon which occurs during any profound heightening of the emotions, such as sexual orgasm, blind anger, mortal terror, consuming grief, etc." (87)

Odin is certainly a master of the use of pain, and Freya as well as demonstrated in the section on their myths related to magical self-transformation and questing for the unknown. The myths identify power with blood, but it is the pain that releases the energy needed while blood carries only the dark antinomian aspect.

Pain is the primary anchoring power in magic. Pain holds consciousness in the moment. Pain reminds you of reality and keeps you from losing yourself in some imaginative visualization or lucid dream. In an attempt to transcend the pain, you will attempt to separate from the world of sensation. Do not allow this to happen. The whole point is to feel the pain and be in the moment with expanded awareness. Pain is also a balancing and empowering factor to ecstasy and fury. Your senses are much more capable of experiencing extremes of pleasure when they have tasted extremes of pain. Inga Steddinger explains it beautifully in *Wiccan Sex-Magic* when she says,

> "On an esoteric or magical level one of the main things about the use of *pain/pleasure* practices in magic is the pattern of *transformation* it sets up. It gets the body programmed, wired, or whatever metaphor you want to use, to create patterns for *changing* things from one form into another. It has been found that such techniques, if they can be accepted naturally, have the potential for unlocking transformative energies more profoundly than any other - because they come from such a deep level in the body/[mind]/soul complex." (4)

To truly understand one you must experience the other. Tempering the will with pain is like sharpening a sword for use in battle. Once appropriate levels of pain are reached it is used to tap the supra-consciousness where its power can be exploited. This brings access to true understanding and knowledge, and an awareness of reality in a way not possible through normal consciousness.

Pain techniques (especially for beginners) should be ones that do not permanently harm the body and also do not hinder the performance of ritual tasks. One of the better ones is using alligator clips that can be moved easily to more sensitive skin once the pain dulls in a particular area. Another method is using hot or cold water. Be careful; in order to create sufficient pain you may accidentally use temperatures damaging to skin, especially when using hot. Cold is less likely to do real harm and it has the advantage of maintaining uncomfortable temperatures longer (i.e., ice). Certain body positions can be utilized as well although this can limit ritual options. A low stance can be extremely painful as the lactic acid builds up in the muscle tissue. Using binding techniques work well but they require a high degree of skill and are best done by another person on you. There is something to be said for this social aspect since it matches the need for other participants like the arts of war and sex. Do not underestimate or ignore our social needs. Striking techniques (such as whipping) can send a stinging pain through the body. It is a very sharp pain but must continually be repeated so may not be practical for regular use unless you have help. It is however somewhat ideal for a beginner and historically has wide usage. The following suggestions can leave permanent marks on the body so are recommended only for the most serious practitioner: tattooing, branding, scarification, and body suspension. Tattooing, scarification, and branding are procedures that produce pain for an extended period. They are not practical for frequent use, however, for obvious reasons but may be considered for extremely important transformative work. They regularly serve as a great reminder to stay Awake if done to a visible body location. Body suspension also leaves permanent marks (relatively minor) but should be considered for its important historical and mythological practices. It is also a pain method that requires the practitioner to stay awake and in the moment (the goal of pain use in ritual). Again I warn you, this is only for the most extreme and skilled practitioner. It is not necessary to achieve exaltation.

The mystic ritual is the next key to true power. Nearly every magical system and religion for that matter, incorporate some forms of ritual. A ritual is a set of practices designed to mimic and command the desired effect in the material world. By its very nature magic is antinomian but for some reason people forget this fact. It is time to throw away the cute little fairy incense burner and the furry stuffed animal totem. Select items for your ritual area that are traditionally consider evil or culturally unacceptable. This heightens the effectiveness. For the ritual setting you need to incorporate all five senses. Crystal Dawn and Dr. Stephen Flowers add "The use of aesthetics, of employing symbolism to appeal to a sense of sexuality, beauty and awesome power, is a key to triggering states of consciousness in which the magician can effectively express his or her will." (3). We can add to this the rituals of Anton Szandor LaVey, as expressed in this quote from *The Satanic Bible*, "There are three types of ceremony incorporated in the practice of Satanic magic... A sex ritual... The second type of ritual is of a compassionate [growth] nature... The third motivating force is that of destruction." (114). These certainly duplicate the three drives, and as such modeling your ritual space to reflect them would definitely be empowering.

Separate your ritual space from the mundane world and your mundane world form your ritual space. It is important to eliminate all non-magical symbols in the area and create an atmosphere like no other. Remove all brand items and advertising media from the area so you don't have anything you don't want entering your subconscious. You don't want to have a coke can in your peripheral vision while performing a personal transformation. Remove all the objects that remind you of someone or something else unless specifically related to the working. All items should be related to or made especially for the task at hand. Sights, sounds, smells, textures, and even tastes should be looked into carefully. Later on this will not be as important, but for a long time and at least until a good deal of mastery is developed it will be absolutely mandatory. Think of consciousness like the visible light spectrum. There are portions that are above and below our perception; we can only perceive a fraction of the full spectrum. Symbols talk to that hidden portion and there are entire bodies of thought encapsulated in a single icon. The three main symbols used for the Dark Arts of Immortality are the Chaos symbol (figure 4), the inverted Valknut (figure 5), and the inverted Pentagram (figure 6). These are great for the ritual chamber.

The Chaos symbol (Art of War) appears as a circle with eight arrows emanating out of it. It represents the power of choice with its arrows showing the effect of your actions on the Universe. It is a good reminder to step beyond the concept of good and evil. Concentrate on what is right and wrong with regard to your personal aim of immortality (renown and self-deification). It also reflects unwanted influences of causality, pushing away ripples in the pond. The Pentacle (Art of Sex) represents both the five senses (visual, auditory, olfactory, gustatory, and kinesthetic) and the cycle of interaction (perceive, process, provide, change, effect). It is a reminder to evaluate everything you perceive and then control how you utilize it. It also suggests to you how you approach those areas in communications with others. The Valknut (Art of Magic) represents the nine components of the Self-complex and the process of self-evolution. It reminds you to focus your intent toward manifesting your

Sal-Odr-Ond triad and fetter that power to your Self in a process of self-deification.

These rituals are not for the timid. Don't forget you are attempting to enter a frenzied supra-conscious state of being, exaltation. This is not a quiet, dreamy meditative practice. As *LaVey* says in *The Satanic Witch*,

> "While performing your ritual, remain as aware as possible that you are doing something naughty, forbidden, possibly even nasty. This is not the time to try to scrape you psyche clean with thoughts of breaking inhibitions and false guilts. This is the time to turn unfounded guilts and inhibitions into an *advantage!*" (238)

Keep in mind that later you will be combining magical triggers with combat and sex so select these in advance and focus on these elements during rituals. It would also be helpful to choose a system of magic that will be easy to cross over into other arts. You should literally become a black magician when doing your ritual. Wear whatever you think a would-be god would wear. Stand, walk, and speak accordingly.

Study the Masters

We have already discussed some of the secrets revealed in Germanic mythology. If you wish to further your study you can do so. Start with the myths and move on to the runes and historical culture. If your interest lies somewhere else, the process is similar. Start with primary sources where possible, the knowledge of their beliefs written by them during the time period, and then move to modern comparative studies. Trust your intuition on some matters but start with facts first. This is the process Huston Smith speaks of when he says,

> "Finally, in both science and religion frontier knowledge is disclosed only through the use of instruments... What are the mystic counterparts of such instruments? Basically they are two, one of which is corporate the other private. For collectivities - tribes, societies, civilizations, traditions- the revealing instruments are Revealed Texts, or, in non-literate societies, the ordering myths that are impounded in stories... There comes a point when the mystic's instrument cannot stop with being external and must become - himself." (114)

You will be the ultimate judge within the framework of the Dark Arts of Immortality what works best for you. The highest form of achievement and flattery is when the student becomes a teacher. That is the wish of all ancient masters and myself. Take what information is available, master it, and then create your own body of work. There is room for many more black magicians in the Universe. The more you help yourself the more you will help Man in general.

There is much to learn in the writings of ancient magicians and alchemists and directly from modern practitioners of Black Magic. Howard Bloom speaks of past practices with "The keepers of the mysteries exude a certainty that through their contact with the invisible world, they are able to solve the problems that to us seem baffling." (123). All ancient cultures exhibited some knowledge of the hidden world and created practices to interact with it. You can save a lot of time if you work with others on the quest who have already accomplished something. Even the masters wasted time and energy pursuing practices that did not serve them well. One of the immediate concerns for the Dark Artist is the emphasis on meditation in past writings. Meditation does have its uses, but there has clearly been an over-emphasis on this practice throughout history. Remember we are at our lowest consciousness when asleep (unconscious). Why would we pursue higher consciousness through a state closer to sleep (meditation) rather than farther away (i.e. excitation)? Balance is the watchword.

Studying the words of the masters on your own is possible and at times the only practicality but it would be best to go to or at least interact with a school of the Left Hand Path (Church of Satan, Temple of Set, Rune-Gild, DAIS, etc.). A school is better able to give you appropriate guidance and help you avoid getting on the wrong path. Another benefit of a school is being around others of like mind. Awakening is hard work and it is nearly impossible to stay Awake all the time. By placing yourself in contact with others that are Awake you can help keep each other from falling back asleep. A word of warning: you should watch out for the modern occultizoid that is not a sovereign in his or her own real life. They are not likely to be much help to you. The people that flock to these organizations are not just the elite, although most of the ones that stay are. You will encounter problems with egos and attitudes from people that think they are the grand poobah. Stay with the established schools and this possibility will be reduced, although not eliminated.

In the immortal words of Anton Szandor LaVey's *Satanic Bible*,

> "This book was written because, with very few exceptions, every tract and paper, every 'secret' grimoire, all the 'great works' on the subject of magic, are nothing more than sanctimonious fraud - guilt-ridden

ramblings and esoteric gibberish by chroniclers of magical lore unable or unwilling to present an objective view of the subject." (21)

He had a certain flair for not mincing words. I tend to be more tactful but certainly not more clear. The reason most of those 'secret grimoires' did not work was the secrets they did not divulge. The magicians of old passed knowledge on through word of mouth. They put the clues in their writing but expected only the initiated to be able to see them. I have given you the missing secrets. The use of your personal ambition and drive for power, coupled with the use of mystic rituals and pain techniques, will push you to the supra-conscious state of being, exaltation. You will experience higher awareness and an altered perception of time. This is the last of the three keys. Now it is time to synthesize them and create a synergistic effect that will propel you to a Divinely Ascended Immortal Soul.

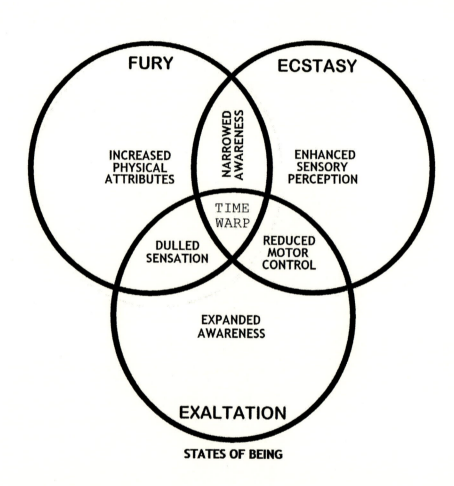

XI. Synergy

The foremost reason that happiness is so hard to achieve is that the universe was not designed with the comfort of humans in mind.
                                           -Mihaly Csikszentmihalyi

What do I mean by synergy? Webster's dictionary defines it as combined action or operation. It is typically used in relation to an increase in sum. In other words you add 3 and 3 and it normally equals 6. With synergistic elements 3 plus 3 would create a 9 effect (like multiplying). A synergistic effect is caused when two items combine and the reaction of the two create a result that is greater than the total sum of the components. You could think of it as multiplying two effects instead of just adding them. It is not an extremely common occurrence in nature, but you might be familiar with this example. Drink a little alcohol and you might get a little tipsy. Take a particular drug and you might get a little woozy. Take them both together and the little tipsy and little woozy multiply exponentially to create a lethal effect. That is synergy.

Combining the Dark Arts of Immortality creates this same type of transformation. If you experience ecstasy you get an increased pleasure threshold, experience fury and you get increased physical attributes, and experience exaltation and you get awareness expansion. All three have an effect on time perception. If you can experience them blended together the synergistic effect on Being will transcend current human limits. If you start using action, speech, and will together you will compound your effect on the Universe. If you start guiding your natural drives toward the same aims and expressions you will harness here-to-fore untapped power. If you fully utilize your powers of perception to create appropriate belief, you will broaden your choices dramatically.

Most of these practices can be done while going about your day-to-day business. As Don Webb explains *"Everything in your life is a Resource. Because of the profound sleep that mankind has, we don't see this. In fact the greatest power against our Becoming a Lord of the Left Hand Path is the fact we don't know what our resources are."* (95). Most of the cycle of interaction can be improved by just becoming aware of it and thinking about its principles as you go about your daily activities. By placing more emphasis on the cycle and making improvements in habit you will make huge synergistic strides toward a better life now and immortality later. The Dark Arts will take care of the rest.

It is paramount that you realize self-development is your responsibility. You have been gifted with a remarkable combination of physiology, psychology, and pneumatology whether from the Gods/esses or evolution makes no difference. The causal Universe is not necessarily looking out for your best interest. We don't have billions of years to work out some grand design. To make the most of your potential you must start now and finish soon. The Dark Arts of Immortality will give you a fuller, longer, and richer quality of life. More than you have now and more than you have ever dreamed possible. Their sound principles also give you a better chance at immortality than any other ideology on the planet. By elevating yourself you help the development of all mankind. The final key to the process is synthesis.

Synthesis

I have covered the divisions of the human being (warrior/lover/mage) in several areas. We have the division in consciousness (subconscious, conscious, and supra-conscious). We have the division in drives (mortido, libido, and physis). We have the divisions in doing (act, speak, and will). We have the divisions in perception (senses, reason, and intuition). We have divisions in the Universe (material, astral, ethereal) and our worlds (objective, subjective, and noujective). All of these combine in Man. All of these can be synthesized into a whole concept of higher Being. Pauli recognized a part of this as Pauwels and Bergier say,

> "'In view of the division of the activities of the human mind into different compartments which have been strictly maintained for centuries,' says *Wolfgang Pauli*, 'I envisage a method whose aim would be to reconcile contraries in a synthesis incorporating a rational understanding and a mystical experience of their unity. No other Objective would be in harmony with the mythology, whether avowed or not, of our epoch.'" (63)

We will take it a step further by reconciling all areas of Being. I will remind you that you have already experienced steps along the way with the "Zone", "Flow", and "Rapture" (peak performance, optimal experience, hyper emotion).

One of the most important elements every reader should take away from this book is the concept of synergizing act, speak, and will. In everything you desire or attempt you should act in such a way as to make it happen, speak in such a way to cause it to occur, and will in such a way as to bring it to fruition. Anyone can practice synergizing those elements without changing anything else in their personal philosophy or theology.

Life is not about conservation of energy. The more you do or use something the more you can do. Muscles don't get weaker when you use them; they get weaker when you don't. The mind doesn't get weaker when you use it; it gets weaker when you don't. By conjecture your spirit won't get weaker by using it, it gets weaker when you don't. In order to give yourself the highest possibility of success you should use all three worlds for everything. This unified practice will project your Self and all you want into the Universe with full force. Using only one method and whining about the lack of results is pure insanity. If you wish to truly change your quality of life at least take this to heart: combine belief with choice and these methods and there is little you cannot accomplish.

Rapture, Flow, Zone

There are currently a few concepts that appear to have elements of supra-consciousness blended together. They are certainly worth studying at least for the common elements they exhibit and the confirmation they provide for the Dark Arts of Immortality. I am speaking here of the "Zone", "Flow", and "Rapture". Each of these can work wonders but they fall short of the mark we have set for personal power now and ascension later. They are great steps but it will be necessary to develop beyond these intermediate stages. However, it is important to have an understanding of them and learn to initiate these regularly. Consider them an intermediate stage of development. It is quite probable if you haven't experienced all of these states before you will encounter and master each on the way to DAIS.

Religious rapture has been the focus of many religious and magical works in the past. It is probably not an experience most average people have encountered. Some may have come close during things like revivals and baptisms but that is about it. It is a near out of body, or at least out of mind sense of oblivion. Historically they were the domains of the ascetic. Monks and priests experimented with ways of altering consciousness. Their practices ranged from days-long meditation to flogging. More modern examples are the Quakers, Shakers, snake dancers, and those who practice speaking in tongues. While there is some merit to their wisdom like hyper activity their methods will not work for us. The Right Hand path they have selected will be counter-productive to our path of self-deification. They lack the antinomian nature of self-empowerment and see the source of power as coming from outside themselves. They lack a true understanding of the human drives. This one-track thinking also tends to make them shun the hard work involved in transforming the Self.

"Flow" is the word coined by *Mihaly Csikszentmihalyi* in his book of the same name. Unlike rapture most people have experienced some form of flow without even realizing it. In his own words,

> "Yet we have all experienced times when, instead of being buffeted by anonymous forces, we do feel in control of our actions, masters of our own fate. On the rare occasions that it happens, we feel a sense of exhilaration; a deep sense of enjoyment that is long cherished and that becomes a landmark in memory for what life should be like. This is what we mean by *optimal experience*." (22)

This 'optimal experience' would be a time when you were working on a favorite hobby (job, craft, recreation, etc.) and everything went perfect. You had a great sense of pleasure and satisfaction from the task and you lost total track of time during the performance. His work is mainly concerned with happiness achieved through experience of flow. There is good information relating to sexual uses and for this alone well worth study. It is geared toward enjoyment of this life like the Dark Arts but lacks the elements of supra-consciousness. It also tends toward a Right Hand path concept of union with the universal flow. Even though he touches on athletic competition we are going to separate flow from that topic. Flow and the zone are different when it comes to Mihaly's *optimal experience* vs. Dr. Garfield's *peak performance*.

The Zone (not the diet program) has been the subject of study for years. Dr. Garfield codified its elements in his work called *Peak Performance*. Athletes have been trying to elevate their game for millennia. The zone is a word athletes use to describe a point in the game when time slows down, the mind accelerates decision making, and every action is executed with perfect precision. It happens for very brief periods and is extremely difficult to repeat. During the experience you seem to be alienated from yourself and the objective world. Again this state has some useful elements but lacks the expansive awareness we seek. The training methods involve meditation, visualization, and relaxation, which run counter to our fury, ecstasy, and exaltation. As I said before, meditation may be a decent practice for some mental training but it lacks the power of ecstatic states. These are tools that help the mind and body somewhat but certainly avoid the supra-conscious benefits. In the sports involved the activity is fast paced and the body is highly active. It would be more beneficial for the athlete to work with the Dark Arts and practice synthesizing the states of being more closely related to their activity. The zone also lacks the spiritual understanding necessary to help ascension. It does get bonus points due to its more Left-Hand Path orientation and because it does promote self empowerment.

In addition to the problems sited above it appears none of the three take the human drives of sex, death, and growth fully into their concepts. They fail to elevate the human being to the levels necessary for immortality. They are worth study as I have said, especially if you remember a peak performance, optimal experience, or hyper emotion. It would be greatly beneficial if you have experienced more than one of these and can recall it. Write them down with as detailed a description as possible. What were you doing just prior? How did you feel during? What was it like? Do you want to do it again? All three do contain the time fluctuation of supra-consciousness. The more frequently you reach altered states the more you will gain control of them. These experiences and elements will give you something to reference when studying them further or to compare with fury, ecstasy, and exaltation as you work with the Dark Arts of Immortality.

Unifying the Schisms

> "The MEANING OF LIFE - this is the eternal subject of human speculations... But if, instead of speculating, men would simply look within themselves, they would see that in actual fact the meaning of life is not, after all, so obscure." (178)
> P. D. OUSPENSKY IN TERTIUM ORGANUM

The Germanic myths and legends guide one toward unification through the Dark Arts of war, sex, and magic. They point to the divine nature within man and the antinomian methods of manifesting it through transgressions of the three functions of society (force, fecundity, sovereignty). We see man as divided between his three worlds. We combine all these into a cycle of interaction with the Universe. All these schisms can be unified into a single divine Being. The process of its attainment is to methodically unify as many elements as possible into our behavior.

Starting with perception you can use all three methods to capture as much information about the Universe as possible. Engaging all five senses starts with conscious awareness of them. This is not that difficult it just requires a little extra focus as you experience life. Next, you need to really evaluate what you perceive for its hidden meaning. There is an old saying, "follow the money." This is a great catch phrase and hint to evaluate the truth behind the evidence. It is sort of like looking for the disease instead of just looking at the symptoms. There are many times in your life when your gut provided information you didn't consider. Now it is time to pay more attention to its noesis.

Processing the information requires an evaluation based on the knowledge gained and balanced against existing belief. Experience is the best teacher if we are smart enough to learn from our mistakes and pay attention to patterned behavior. Take the time and effort necessary to experience more aspects of life. Try new things. Most people are slack in this regard. Start paying attention to your life lessons. Someone once said insanity is doing the same thing over and over again and expecting different results. You get the idea. Balancing these experiences with superior consciousness would be paramount to maximal learning. Now that you have an understanding of how the Dark Arts contribute to the experiencing of a portion of supra-consciousness and being it is time for you to practice them. Repeated exposure to altered states will slowly allow whole consciousness to merge with full human potential.

Another area that can create a synergistic effect is the drives Libido, Mortido, and Physis. We constantly build up tensions related to each drive. Sometimes people substitute releases of one drive as an attempt to alleviate tensions created by another one. This sometimes works to a marginal degree. Understanding these tensions in relation to the processing of information and belief is necessary to proper learning as well. You must be aware of where your balance of tensions comes from since it impacts mental functioning and spiritual strength. Some of the most powerful synergistic effects are when more than one or all three drives can be directed toward accomplishing the same goal. Why do you think two people fighting over the same lover is so common (and so fierce)? The combatants have combined the sex drive, death drive, and possibly even the growth drive together and focused them on one aim.

Producing has been covered in depth already. Act, speak, and will are necessary to producing the greatest impact on reality. Do not ignore either of the three when trying to work your intent on the Universe. Repeated combined use of these creates an effect similar to exercise. The habitual enactment and use will strengthen them all. Working in concert with belief and the power of choice you can escalate your personal influence in the world.

By repeatedly experiencing fury, ecstasy, and exhalation you will be able to blend the benefits and eliminate the disadvantages by synergistic effect.

The reaching of this new state (DAIS) fights entropy by harnessing power not normally available and gives a new perception of time. This is a sure sign that we are on our way to immortality. By achieving this greater Awakening you will make a name for yourself that will satisfy the need for renown. By teaching others or passing on this ability genetically you will help the species. The schism in consciousness needs to be mended in order to exploit the other 90% of our potential. There is no telling to what height humanity may rise once able to hold the supra-conscious state of Being.

Ultimate Warrior, Lover, Mage

We are a tripartite being seeking unification. We are the Warrior, the Lover, and the Mage all rolled into one. We have lost sight of this fact and our true potential goes to waste. One of the ways you can patch the schism is to merge the patterns of the warrior, lover, and mage within your everyday behavior. Unify these paradigms under a single unique identity: yours. The other method to incorporate will be to combine some of the Dark Arts practices with each other. The first and easiest to combine is magic with sex. Sex-magic practices have been around for centuries. Crystal Dawn and Dr. Flowers explain their use with the following:

> "Therefore the way to increase or give rise to sexual energy is simply to *generate* it in ways the individual finds most pleasurable and appealing. From a practical point of view the main thing about sex-magic is that it works on the basis of sexual energy or arousal. *The higher the level of arousal or excitement, the more sexual energy the magician will have to work with.*" (3)

Combining elements of magical symbolism with martial practices has also been around for a long time. It likewise raises a form of energy that is extremely powerful. Both are very effective techniques. War and sex combine in the sex-duel as discussed earlier. Fighting for attention and satisfaction from a member of the opposite sex is questionably the most dangerous combination but athletes perform this very feat in a safe forum every day. These practices definitely have a synergizing effect. The powers of the philosopher/priest king will multiply with the powers of the lover and in turn multiply with the powers of the warrior in this lifetime by unifying drives toward singular aims. There are several works on sex-magic practices that can be useful for the aspiring artist. Use of magical tattooing or weapon marking are also simple but effective practices. And of course competing in any conflict where sexual reward is possible is helpful. There are many variations that will allow the drives to be combined.

What would be the accomplished Dark Artist's capabilities? His physical attributes would be at a preternatural level. He would thrive in perpetual bliss. His awareness would constantly be expanded beyond normal limits. He would perceive, process and provide much faster due to the time distortion within which he lives. He would be able to control how he affected the dimensions and in turn how they affected him. Results of his interaction with the Universe would be in line with his intent. Events would only affect him in line with his wishes. His actions would be flawless, his speech effective, and his will unimaginable. In order to achieve this level of ability, just having had ecstatic experiences is not enough. The apex of human potential can only be achieved by blending the Dark Arts of war, sex, and magic into a pathway through peak performance, optimal experience, and hyper emotion. The advantages gained through each of the states of being are necessary to override the disadvantages of the others. It should be obvious by now that this zenith of power leads directly to a Divinely Ascended Immortal Soul.

As I explained before, these synergistic effects are extremely powerful and should be sought as frequently as practical. You are a warrior, a lover, and a mage. You do not turn any of these aspects on and off. They are parts of your nature and should be utilized in every aspect. You are the Dark Artist of Immortality.

XII. Conclusions

*If there should exist an end which is desirable for its own sake,
which determines and motivates all other actions and choices,
this end would be that which is absolutely good.
Knowledge of this good would be of great value,
for it would provide an aim for life and a standard by which
to evaluate all other activities and thoughts.*
   -Aristotle

We may quibble over his use of the term 'absolute good' but not the heart of what he said. The point he was trying to make was that if you select a goal for your life that is desirable for its own sake it would be a way to gage all other actions. If those actions helped you achieve that aim they were right if not they were wrong. The purpose of this work suggests the aims of personal evolution, immortality, racial survival, and spiritual eugenics.

This work is both science and art. The repeatable processes explained in this book will give you measurable results and immediate feedback. That is the science. The art is how you make this material uniquely your own through practice.

You have seen how the consciousness and its individual functions are divided. You have seen the vast amount of processes the subconscious can handle through its absorbing of information and hidden controls, thus leaving the rest of the mind to work on other things. We have seen how the conscious mind can analyze current information, create new ideas, and train the self in different tasks. With the achievement of supra-consciousness you can elevate the body, mind, and spirit to ever more perfect levels of Being.

Depending on the definition you select the concept of self-realization can be misleading. But make no mistake Self-realization is the highest aim for each man and woman. Self-realization in metaphysical terms (and as used here) is not about changing one thing into another. It really means a full manifestation of existing potential. If you want to transform your appearance you are really just manifesting an already existing conditional possibility. Unfortunately, most people don't know the extent of those possibilities. Very few humans even come close to manifesting their full capabilities. Becoming immortal is a process of manifesting an already existing potential within the nature of humanity. Self-realization requires knowledge of what you want, belief it is possible, plans for attaining it, and the work to make it happen. Leaving out even one element will eliminate the possibility of your desire occurring.

Ascension

It should be clear by now the ultimate aim of humanity is to ascend into a higher form of Being. Our nature channeled through the drives pushes us ever onward toward this higher existence and identity continuation. Our physiology, psychology, and pneumatology yearn for this like nothing else. The reason we created religion in the first place was to satisfy our desire for continued identity survival after physical death. Our theologies hint at its reality. Our philosophies argue for the possibility. Our science measures its probability. Every form of knowledge man has achieved and codified has sought some aspect of life after death.

We want to believe in an afterlife. The question is what type of immortality do you want to have? Do you wish to serve some cosmic entity? Or do you wish to become your own divine Being? With all the clues available throughout all cultures pointing to personal enlightenment and divine ascension why would anyone practice a system that did not promote such personal power? Why grovel at the feet of some higher power for table scraps? A study of mythology shows the Gods/esses granted us this greater possibility and left instructions for its attainment. A study of evolution shows us we are striving for self-realization as well, and it is built into our own nature as a consequence. It would be stupidity not to follow the Dark Arts of Immortality to their ultimate conclusion; the realization of an independent Divinely Ascended Immortal Soul.

Time and Entropy Revisited

The only know methodology to combat the two enemies of immortality namely time and entropy are the Dark Arts of Immortality. Regardless of your previous beliefs about immortality, the Dark Arts are the best path to follow and they can be incorporated into most existing belief systems. These arts of personal combat, sexual fantasy, and mystic ritual will build a powerful Self in this world no matter what your current situation or philosophy. By conjecture it will lead to a better afterlife. To blindly think you will be rewarded in the afterlife by living a crappy life now is ludicrous. If you believe in reincarnation then our discussions about naming and renown and their relationship to supra-consciousness and Being should strike a cord. If you believe you will come back then developing a powerful self with the Dark Arts of Immortality will help your cycle of rebirth.

If you believe in the possibility of a permanent physical existence then the Dark Arts of Immortality are perfect for you. No other science comes close to elevating Man's life here. It has already been pointed out how magic (in fact all three Dark Arts) extends life. Since higher states of being are achieved through the Dark Arts that change time perception and combat entropy, it is the only known method to have a chance at creating physical immortality. Spiritual transformation can use some of the reasoning above as well. If you are going to build awareness strong enough to survive beyond death of the physical body then nothing empowers the Self, consciousness, and Being like the Dark Arts. The Dark Arts of Immortality are the secret keys to the creation of a Divinely Ascended Immortal Soul.

DAIS is an organization descended from the Harii and founded on the principles of *The Dark Arts of Immortality: Transformation Through War, Sex & Magic*. Its aim is to fully articulate and express their enactment in the Universe through the secrets of *The Nine Doctrines of Darkness*. DAIS, PO Box 56384, Houston, TX 77256-6384. www.thedarkartsofimmortality.com.

Yes indeed, the works of men of genius do follow them, and remain as a lasting treasure. And though there may be disputes and discussions about the immortality of the body or the soul, nobody can deny the immortality of genius, which ever remains as a bright and guiding star to the struggling humanities of succeeding ages.

-VATSYAYANA

Partial Reading List / Bibliography

The Varieties of Religions Experience - William James

Origins of the Sacred: The Ecstasies of Love and War - Dudley Young

The Will to Power - Friedrich Nietzsche - Translation by Walter Kaufmann and R.J Hollingdale

Forgotten Truth - Huston Smith

The Psychology of C. G. Jung - By Jolande Jacobi

Studia Germanica Vol. 1 - Dr. Stephen E. Flowers

Scientology: The Fundamentals of Thought - L. Ron Hubbard

The Psychology of Man's Possible Evolution - P. D. Ouspensky

The Lucifer Principle - Howard Bloom

For a Philosophy of Freedom and Strife - Gunter Figal - Translated by Wayne Klein

Heidegger: an Introduction - Richard Polt

The Morning of the Magicians - Louis Pauwels & Jacques Bergier

Man Into Wolf - Robert Eisler

The English Warrior from earliest times to 1066 - Stephen Pollington

The Metaphysics of the Matrix - Jorge J. E. Gracia and Jonathan J. Sanford

Neo-Materialism and the Death of the Subject - Daniel Barwick

Notes for Underground: Nihilism and The Matrix - Thomas S. Hibbs

The Paradox of Real Response to Neo-Fiction - Sarah E. Worth

The Sweet Spot in Time - By John Jerome

Warrior Speed - Ted Weimann

Spec Ops: Case Studies in Special Operations Warfare: Theory and Practice - William H. McRaven

Witchdom of the True - Edred Thorsson

Tertium Organum - P. D. Ouspensky

Blood Rites: Origins and History of the Passions of War - Barbara Ehrenreich

Book 4 - Aleister Crowley

Liber Null & Pshychonaut: An Introduction to Chaos Magic - Peter J. Carroll

At the Well of Wyrd - Edred Throsson

Runelore: A Handbook of Esoteric Runology - Edred Thorsson

Parallel Universes: The Search for Other Worlds - Fred Alan Wolf

The Agricola and the Germania - Tacitus - Translated by H. Mattingly - Revised Translation by S. A. Handford

Liber Kaos - Peter J. Carroll

Hermetic Magic - Dr. Stephen E. Flowers

Uncle Setnakt's Essental Guide to the Left Hand Path - Don Webb

Wiccan Sex-Magic - Inga Steddinger

The New Flesh Palladium - Robert North

Carnal Alchemy: A Sado-Magical Exploration of Pleasure, Pain and Self-Transformation - Crystal Dawn and Stephen E. Flowers

The Kama Sutra of Vatsyayana - Translated by Sir Richard Burton and F. F. Arbuthnot

Light *Her* Fire - Ellen Kreidman

Fire and Ice - Dr. Stephen E. Flowers

Gods and Myths of Northern Europe - H. R. Ellis Davidson

Basic Teachings of the Great Philosphers - S. E. Frost, Jr.

The Art of Seduction - Robert Greene

Destiny of the Warrior - Geroges Dumezil

The Cult of Othin - H. M. Chadwick

The Nordic Legacy - unknown

The Viking Road to Byzantium - H. R. Ellis-Davidson

The Code of the Warrior - Rick Fields

The Occult Experience - Nevill Drury

Unholy Alliance - Peter Lavenda

Pacts With the Devil - S. Jason Black & Christopher S. Hyatt, Ph.D.

Black Runa - Dr. Stephen E. Flowers

Red Runa - Dr. Stephen E. Flowers

Necronomicon - "Mad Arab" - Abdul Alhazred

Satan Wants You - Arthur Lyons

The Satanic Bible - Anton Szandor LaVey

The Devil's Notebook - Anton Szandor LaVey

The Satanic Witch - Anton Szandor LaVey

Flow: The Psychology of Optimal Experience - Mihaly Csikszentmihalyi

The Occult Experience - Nevill Drury

Unholy Alliance - Peter Lavenda

Pacts With the Devil - S. Jason Black & Christopher S. Hyatt, Ph.D.

Black Runa - Dr. Stephen E. Flowers

Red Runa - Dr. Stephen E. Flowers

Necronomicon - "Mad Arab" - Abdul Alhazred

Satan Wants You - Arthur Lyons

The Satanic Bible - Anton Szandor LaVey

The Devil's Notebook - Anton Szandor LaVey

The Satanic Witch - Anton Szandor LaVey

Printed in the United States
58202LVS00003B/269